RELAX IN THE CITY
week by week

RELAX IN THE CITY
week by week

52 practical skills to help you
beat stress and find peace

Allen Elkin Ph.D.

dbp

DUNCAN BAIRD PUBLISHERS
LONDON

To my wife Beth—my best friend; and to our children
Josh and Katy, who bring us so much joy.

Relax in the City Week by Week
Allen Elkin Ph.D.

First published in the United Kingdom
and Ireland in 2004 by
Duncan Baird Publishers Ltd
Sixth Floor
Castle House
75–76 Wells Street
London W1T 3QH

Conceived, created and designed by
Duncan Baird Publishers

Managing Editors: Judy Barratt and Julia Charles
Editor: Ingrid Court-Jones
Managing Designer: Manisha Patel
Designer: Megan Smith

Library of Congress Cataloging-in-Publication Data available

ISBN: 1-84483-056-X

10 9 8 7 6 5 4 3 2 1

Typeset in Apollo and Trade Gothic
Colour reproduction by Scanhouse, Malaysia
Printed in Thailand by Imago

PUBLISHER'S NOTE
Before following any advice or
practice suggested in this book,
it is recommended that you consult
your doctor as to its suitability,
especially if you suffer from
any health problems or special
conditions. The publishers
and the author cannot accept
responsibility for any injuries
or damage incurred as a result
of following the exercises in this
book, or of using the relaxation
techniques described or
mentioned here.

Contents

Introduction

For many years now I have lived in a big city, but this wasn't always the case. I fondly remember the several years I spent living and working in a small Canadian town. Looking back now, my life there seems so relaxed and effortless. The rhythms of life were simpler and gentler; the pace was slower and the frustrations fewer. Life was just easier.

I can also remember the shock of moving from that small town to a much larger city. It soon became clear that urban life was very different. I was stunned by the number of people in the streets, the noise of traffic, the less-than-pleasant smells and the frequent incivility of the people. I quickly became aware of the dangers and of just how expensive living there could be. But most of all I missed the peace and tranquility that I had enjoyed, and taken for granted, in that small town. In short, I found that living in the city can be very stressful.

Yet, at the same time I also found myself enjoying city life. I liked the vitality and excitement. I valued the ethnic diversity and cultural opportunities. I still get great pleasure from exploring new neighborhoods and discovering a wonderful off-the-beaten-track restaurant, bakery, or bookstore. I like meeting new people. I like having choices. I love the energy of the city.

Indeed, on good days there can be much to like about city life. Conversely, on bad days the strains of urban life can be draining and make you wonder why you stay there. Many city-dwellers live with this feeling of ambivalence. They would enjoy the city so much more if they could cope better with its demands and frustrations. Unfortunately, cities do not come with a user's manual. We need help. We need a road map, a guide to help us relax and find contentment, while still enjoying all that the city has to offer.

In these pages I will show you how you can cope better with the stress and hassles of city life. You will learn how to develop more stress-resilient thinking styles. You will find out how to relax your body and quieten your mind, and how to relieve tension and free yourself from worry. You will also discover how to create your own personal oasis, your refuge from the hustle and bustle of the city.

Finding peace in the city entails beginning a personal voyage of inner discovery as you build a repertoire of new skills and behaviors. This book will help you master those skills and acquire the practical tools that will allow you to transform your urban life into a more joyful, more satisfying, and altogether more tranquil experience. Learning how to relax in the city starts here.

Getting Started

A Chinese proverb tells us, "A journey of a thousand miles begins with a single step." You've taken that first step in starting to read this book. The proverb's author might have added that you want to be sure that your first step is in the right direction. The same wisdom holds true as you begin your journey on the road to learning how to cope with the pressures and demands of urban living. You need to set out with the proper gear—an accurate road map, a good compass, and the right attitude.

In this chapter you start off in the right direction by exploring what urban stress looks like and where it comes from. You learn many of the valuable tools and skills you need to reduce and manage that stress, such as how to relax your body and still your mind. In short, you discover how to eliminate, or certainly minimize, the distressing factors that can detract from your enjoyment of life in the city.

Understanding Stress

You've probably heard the word "stress" a thousand times, yet if you were pressed to explain the term you might find yourself stuck. Defining stress is much like defining happiness. Everyone knows what it is, but it's hard to come up with a good definition. So here is a simple, yet useful way of understanding stress.

Think of stress as the feelings you experience when you face an event or a situation that you perceive as challenging your ability to cope. For example, if you perceive an event or a situation as mildly challenging, you feel only a little stress. However, if you perceive that same event or situation as overwhelming, you feel a great deal of stress. The amount of stress you feel reflects the difference between the demands of the event or situation and how effectively you feel you can cope with it. For example, waiting in line at the bank when you have all the time in the world triggers little stress. But, waiting in line when you are running late for an important appointment triggers much more stress.

When you live in a city, there is no shortage of circumstances that can cause stress. Whenever you have too many people living, working, and playing in too small a space, and all trying to do roughly the same things at about the same time, you are bound to have problems. There is too much noise, too much congestion, too much conflict, too much danger, too much expense—too much of just about everything. And that's not all.

If you look below the surface, you can find more subtle sources of stress in the city. For one thing, you experience uncertainty and unpredictability, because you never know what is going to happen next. Living in a city means having to suffer and deal with hassles on a day-to-day basis. It could be as simple as having to wait what seems like interminably for your bus to work, or being awakened at three o'clock in the morning by the wailing of a car alarm, or getting stuck in traffic and missing your flight. The problem is that many aspects of city life are beyond our control. And when we lack control, we feel stressed.

Then, of course, there is the emotional isolation. Cities seem to be full of strangers. It is quite likely that you will not know many of the people who live next door, or in your block, or even in the actual building where you live. Despite being surrounded by people, you can feel very alone living in a city, and this can be extremely stressful. Meeting others may *seem* easy, but often in practice it is not. Becoming part of a neighborhood and a community takes a lot of time and effort—all of which can add to your stress levels.

Often, our discontent with the city is caused by daily hassles, such as a lack of a parking spaces, traffic gridlock, clueless taxi drivers, salespeople with attitude, overcrowded restaurants, dogs running around off the leash, people shouting down cell phones in public places, and so on. When you take a closer look at city hassles, you become aware of two things: first, there are *lots* of them; and second, the same ones happen *over* and *over* again.

When you come up against a relentless succession of hassles, you can suffer from what I call "urban strain." Most of us can handle one, two, and maybe three or four hassles in quick succession. But when the number is even higher, we can quickly become overwhelmed and even feel totally defeated. The ironic thing is that we usually deal pretty well with life's big problems—the major sources of stress, such as bereavements, illness, divorce, financial setbacks, and so on. Somehow big problems summon up resources hidden deep within us. We rise to each demand, calling upon some hitherto undiscovered inner strength, and we manage to cope. It's the little things that get to us—the petty annoyances, the small frustrations, and the minor irritations that ultimately make us feel chronically stressed. It is the everyday hassles of the city that become the real enemy.

IDENTIFY YOUR URBAN STRESS

The first step in coping with stress in the city is to recognize its causes. Using a scale where 0 = no stress, 1 = minor stress, 2 = moderate stress, and 3 = major stress, rate how stressful you find the items listed below. Then add up your score to gauge your overall urban stress level.

- *crime*
- *danger*
- *noise*
- *graffiti*
- *dirty streets*
- *vermin*
- *garbage*
- *bad smells*

- *polluted air*
- *high cost of living*
- *fast pace*
- *overcrowding*
- *rude people*
- *inconsiderate neighbors*
- *lack of privacy*

- *cramped living space*
- *unfriendliness*
- *foul language*
- *the homeless*
- *panhandlers*
- *traffic congestion*
- *lack of parking*

- *bad drivers*
- *unreliable public transportation*
- *waiting in lines*
- *children's safety*
- *limited space for children to play in*
- *not enough parks*

Your urban stress total

Your score	*Your urban stress level*
0 to 9	*much below average*
10 to 39	*below average*
40 to 69	*average*
70 to 99	*above average*
100 and above	*much above average*

Stress and Your Body

Your body is a prime target for stress. To understand why, you need to cast your mind back to a situation that might have faced one of your ancestors, millions of years ago. Imagine them roaming about looking for something to eat when they spot a tiger (which also happens to be looking for something to eat). Your ancestor reacts with an innate survival response—their "fight-or-flight" mechanism kicks in. Their body floods with epinephrine (adrenaline) and their mind becomes ultra-alert—they are now primed either to fight the tiger or to run away. This reaction to stress was, and still is, nature's way of preparing us to deal with danger. Stress, way back when, was nature's way of keeping us alive.

Of course, it is highly unlikely that you will ever encounter a tiger in the city. These days our stress tends to come in more mundane forms—we are more likely to become stressed from an encounter with a rude salesperson or an angry driver. However, your body responds to these minor problems in much the same way as it would if you were facing a life-threatening danger. You experience a dramatic series of physiological changes that ready you for the emergency. When your body releases the hormone epinephrine into the bloodstream, your heart rate speeds up. Your blood pressure rises. You breathe more rapidly. Your nostrils flare, allowing you to take in more air. Your digestion slows. Blood is directed away from your skin and internal organs and is shunted to your brain and skeletal muscles where it might imminently be needed. Your muscles tense. You feel stronger and you are ready for action. Your body gets ready to repair any damage that you might sustain, and your pupils dilate so that you can see better. Clearly, stress has helped the human race to adapt so that we maximize our potential for survival.

However, when mundane situations trigger the "fight-or-flight" response day after day, year after year, our health often pays the price. The signs and symptoms of stress can range from the harmless to the dramatic—from simply feeling extra-tired to suffering a heart attack. Stress can play a role in exacerbating the symptoms of a wide variety of other disorders and illnesses. When you are under stress, your muscles contract and they become tense. This muscle tension can affect your nerves, blood vessels, organs, skin, and bones. Chronically tense muscles can result in a variety of conditions and disorders, including muscle spasms, cramps, pain in the jaw or face, teeth-grinding, and tremors. Many forms of headache, chest pain, and back pain are also caused by stress-induced muscle tension.

Stress can play a role in coronary heart disease, cardiac arrests, and strokes. This is not surprising, because it can not only increase your blood pressure, but also constrict your blood vessels, raise your cholesterol levels, and trigger arrhythmia. Stress is now considered a major risk factor in heart disease, right up there with smoking, obesity, and a lack of exercise.

Your gastro-intestinal system can also be adversely affected by stress, which stimulates the secretion of acid in your stomach and can speed up or slow down digestion. Constipation, diarrhea, flatulence, and bloating can all be stress-related. And stress can aggravate reflux, colitis, and irritable bowel syndrome.

The other crucial bodily function that stress attacks is the immune system, making it less effective in resisting bacteria and viruses. Stress may also play a role in exacerbating immune-system disorders, such as HIV and AIDS, herpes, rheumatoid arthritis, certain allergies, and other auto-immune conditions.

Of course, not everyone suffers from serious stress-related conditions, but now that you are aware of the affect that stress *could* have on your body, you may wish to learn how to minimize and manage your own stress. The first steps are to analyze how stress affects you and to assess just how stressed you are.

MEASURE YOUR URBAN STRESS

Using a scale where 0 = never, 1 = sometimes, 2 = often, 3 = very often, rate the frequency with which you've experienced the symptoms listed below in the last two weeks. Then add up your score to gauge your overall stress symptom total.

- *pounding heart*
- *tightness in chest*
- *increased perspiration*
- *rapid breathing*
- *aching shoulders*
- *lower-back pain*
- *hives or skin rash*
- *headaches*
- *colds or 'flu*
- *stomach discomfort*
- *diarrhea or constipation*

- *biting your nails*
- *twitches or tics*
- *nausea*
- *loss of appetite*
- *overeating*
- *excessive drinking*
- *excessive smoking*
- *excessive spending*
- *feeling depressed*
- *feeling helpless*
- *increased anxiety*

- *increased irritability*
- *increased anger*
- *impatience*
- *restlessness*
- *lack of energy*
- *fatigue or tiredness*
- *difficulty concentrating*
- *forgetfulness*
- *bouts of crying*
- *loss of sexual interest*
- *sleep difficulties*

Your stress symptom total

Your score	***Your stress symptom level***
0–19	*Lower than average*
20–39	*Average*
40–49	*Moderately high*
50 and above	*Much higher than average*

Learning How to Relax

Learning how to calm your body and how to still your mind are important tools with which to reverse the stress response and return to a more relaxed state. By knowing how to let go of bodily tension and free your mind of distressing thoughts, you can minimize many of the negative consequences of stress.

In this book you will be introduced to a variety of relaxation methods. Some will work better for you than others. The idea is to discover and use those that work best for *you*.

Of course, some relaxation techniques may take a little getting used to. For example, you might think that breathing exercises are "not your thing." Yet, if you persevere and master the basic techniques, you may be pleasantly surprised. When I first began exploring various methods to relieve stress, I felt lukewarm about meditation. Now I swear by it. So, do keep an open mind.

Most of the techniques described in this book require you to practice before you can master them. The trick is to try out the methods one at a time and not tackle them all at once. Pick one of the relaxation exercises and set aside 15 to 20 minutes each day for a week to practice. If, after seven days you don't feel comfortable with it, leave it and try a different one. Once you find techniques that you like, use them regularly and make them part of your life.

DO A ONE-MINUTE BODY-SCAN

One of the best ways of learning how to recognize bodily tension is to do this simple one-minute exercise. Once you get used to scanning your body for tension, you will be able to do it whenever you have a spare moment in your hectic schedule, such as while you are waiting in a traffic jam.

1. Sit or lie down somewhere comfortable. Close your eyes.

2. Start your body-scan by asking yourself: Are there any signs of tightness or discomfort anywhere in my body? Notice any parts that seem a bit cramped or uncomfortable or any areas in which you feel pain.

3. Now scan your body in a more systematic way. Start with the top of your head and work your way down to your toes, asking yourself the following questions: Is my brow furrowed? Are my eyebrows knitted? Is my jaw clenched? Are my lips pursed? Are my shoulders hunched? Are my arms tense? Are my thigh and calf muscles tight? Are my toes curled?

4. Repeat the scan 2 or 3 times a day or whenever you can. With a little practice, you will be able to scan your whole body in less than a minute.

Relaxing Your Body

In many of us, stress manifests in our muscles. When you are under stress, your muscles tighten slowly and often imperceptibly. Over time tension sets in. You may not notice this tension until you feel tired, get a headache, or feel sore in your neck or shoulders. Learning how to release tight muscles enables you to benefit from true physical relaxation. But there other benefits: your breathing slows and deepens, your heart rate falls, and your mind clears. Being totally relaxed makes every part of you feel good.

There are several ways to relax your muscles. A good technique is Progressive Muscle Relaxation, in which you systematically relax the major muscle groups of your body, one after the other. Using this approach you first tense your muscles, and then relax them completely. By purposely tightening them in this way, you are able to recognize what muscle tension feels like and to identify which muscles tense up.

Begin progressive relaxation by tensing a specific muscle or group of muscles (for example, in your neck, your shoulders, your arms, and so on). Don't tense the muscles as hard as you can, just use about three-quarters of your strength, and always stop if you feel any pain. When you have tensed and relaxed all the major muscle groups in your body, you will feel much less stressed.

LET GO OF TENSION

When tension builds up in your muscles, your body can't function at an optimal level. This exercise will help you to relax your muscles whenever they feel tight.

1. Find a quiet place where you can sit comfortably and remain undisturbed. Close your eyes. Try to clear your mind.

2. Make a fist with your right hand and at the same time bend your elbow, flexing your arm muscles. Hold for about 10 seconds, then relax for 15 to 20 seconds before repeating with your left hand and arm.

3. Raise your right foot so that you tense your right thigh and buttock. Hold this tension for 10 seconds and then release it, letting your leg relax back down to the floor. Repeat this sequence with your left leg and foot.

4. Wrinkle your forehead by raising your eyebrows. Hold for about 10 seconds, and then let go for 15 to 20 seconds. Next, clench your jaw by biting down on your back teeth and forcing a smile. Hold for about 10 seconds, and then relax your jaw, letting your mouth fall slightly ajar. Now, bend your head forward for 10 seconds. Relax and straighten your head. Scrunch up your shoulders for 10 seconds, then relax them.

5. Take a deep breath and hold that breath for about 10 seconds, tensing the muscles in your stomach. Now relax and breathe out.

6. Open your eyes as you feel more relaxed and refreshed. Repeat this exercise several times a day, and whenever your body feels tense.

The Breath that Calms

You probably take your breathing for granted. And why not? After all, you've been breathing for years now. What you may not know is that changing your breathing patterns is one of the easiest and best ways of releasing tension and relieving stress. You simply have to learn how to breathe the right way.

When you were an infant, proper breathing came naturally. As you grew up, you probably lost this ability somewhere along the way. Like many people, you may now be a chest-and-shoulder breather, bringing air into your lungs by expanding your chest cavity and raising your shoulders. You may also habitually hold your breath, stopping your breathing entirely when you're alarmed, distracted, or lost in thought. Both are inefficient, stress-producing ways to breathe.

Your breathing patterns deteriorate even more when you are under stress or in emotional distress. At such times your breathing becomes faster and shallower. Less oxygen enters your bloodstream and reaches your brain. Your blood vessels constrict. Your heart rate and your blood pressure go up and you may feel light-headed, shaky, and more tense. To make things worse, once your breathing goes awry, you feel even more stressed. The whole process can become a distressing cycle. And when you are feeling extremely stressed, upset, or emotional, you hyperventilate and breathe out too much carbon dioxide. Over-breathing in this way can cause panic attacks, fainting, and dizziness.

Simply by changing your breathing patterns, you can rapidly induce a state of greater relaxation. If you control the way you breathe, you have a powerful tool for reducing bodily tension. As important, you have a tool that helps prevent your body from becoming tense in the first place. Breathing provides your body with oxygen and removes waste products—primarily carbon dioxide—from your blood. Your lungs carry out this gas exchange. Lungs, however, do not have their own muscles for breathing. Your diaphragm is the major muscle necessary for proper breathing. The diaphragm is a dome-shaped muscle that separates your chest cavity from your abdominal cavity, and acts as a flexible floor for your lungs.

When you inhale, your diaphragm flattens downward, opening up more space in your chest cavity, and permitting your lungs to inflate fully. When you exhale, your diaphragm returns to its dome shape. Diaphragmatic, or abdominal breathing provides the most efficient way of expelling carbon dioxide and taking in oxygen.

Your diaphragm works automatically, but you can override the process, especially when you are under stress. And that's when problems can arise. Too often you neglect to use your diaphragm properly when you breathe, and you interfere with the proper exchanges of gases in your pulmonary system, which can result in greater tension, more fatigue, and more stress. Relaxing your breathing means slowing it down and learning to breathe more deeply, using your diaphragm fully.

I often find that people who want to adopt new breathing patterns also have a fervent desire to ensure that they master the new ways perfectly. They frequently get so lost in concentrating on their body properly or the mechanics of how their lungs work that they wind up more stressed than they were before they started. Don't let this happen to you. Bear in mind that there is no one correct way in which to breathe all the time. Give yourself lots of room to experiment with your breathing. And don't overdo it. If you've been breathing inefficiently for many years, changing gears may take some time. You are not taking a test, so don't grade yourself on how deep you can breathe or how flat you can make your diaphragm. After all, the goal is to relax, not to become even more stressed.

TRY ZEN BREATHING

Zen breathing is a technique that helps you to breathe slowly, deeply, and more efficiently, and to maximize your lung capacity. Once you master how to breathe correctly in this way, you'll find that it's a great aid to relaxation.

1. *Lie comfortably on your bed, in a reclining chair, or on a rug. Keep your knees bent and your legs slightly apart. If you wish, close your eyes.*

2. *Put your left hand on your abdomen near your navel, and your right hand on your chest. Notice the motion of your breathing. Try to relax and let go of any tension you feel in your body.*

3. *Slowly inhale through your nose, taking the air down to the bottom of your lungs. Notice your left hand rising slightly on your abdomen. Your right hand placed on your chest should move very little—and when it does, should move only after your abdomen has risen.*

4. *Part your lips and exhale slowly, emptying your lungs from top to bottom. Make a whooshing sound as the air passes out through your mouth. Notice your left hand on your abdomen fall.*

5. *Pause slightly, then inhale and repeat the breathing cycle. Continue to breathe in this way for about 10 minutes or until you feel relaxed and peaceful.*

Relaxing Your Mind

To be completely relaxed, you need not only to release tension from your body, but also to calm your mind. For many people, stress takes the form of psychological or mental distress. If this applies to you, you may find that your mind is filled with distressing thoughts that stop you from relaxing. Any kind of worry can cause you great stress. You may be anxious about losing your job (perhaps because you have heard rumors that your company is being taken over and down-sized). Or maybe you are concerned about your health because your hectic social life involves a lot of drinking in bars; or, then again, perhaps the high cost of urban living is getting you down. Whatever the source of your anxiety, you are clearly not going to relax until you stop—or at least diminish—this mental mayhem.

There are many ways to calm your mind and eliminate worrisome thoughts. Some people find it helpful to listen to some mellow music or a recording of natural sounds, such as birdsong or the crashing of waves onto the seashore. Others find it effective to use their imagination (see exercise, opposite). If you can focus your mind on relaxing or soothing sounds or images, your mind will slow, and this will make your stress level fall dramatically.

VISUALIZE CALM

This simple visualization exercise will help to you to relax your body and to banish anxious thoughts, so that you can experience your day-to-day life feeling rested and refreshed.

1. *Find a place where you won't be disturbed for several minutes. Sit in a favorite chair or lie down so that you feel as comfortable as possible. Close your eyes and breathe slowly and deeply. Let any tension drain from your muscles—try to let go totally.*

2. *Now use your imagination to transport you to a beautiful beach on a tropical island. The weather is perfect. Lying on the silver sand, you feel the warm breeze caress your body and you can smell the scent of your coconut suntan lotion. You hear the lapping of the waves as they reach the shore and the rustling of the palm trees. As you sip a cocktail of exotic fresh fruit juices, you gaze idly out to sea. You are completely relaxed. Your mind is totally at peace. You feel wonderful.*

3. *Immerse yourself in your visualization, allowing it to relax you completely. Use all your senses to bring the scene to life. Notice the details of your surroundings. Feel the sand between your toes; taste the salt in the air. By using all your senses you can enrich your image and make it more effective as a vehicle for relaxation.*

4. *Let yourself drift into a deeply relaxed state. When you feel completely refreshed, slowly open your eyes and become aware of your real surroundings again—safe in the knowledge that you can escape back to your paradise beach whenever you wish.*

The best image is one that helps create feelings of calm and tranquility. It might be a memory from your childhood, or a mental picture from a particularly relaxing vacation, or merely a place in your own imagination. It might be walking in a quiet forest, lying under a tree in the park, or perhaps soaking in an aromatherapy bath, scented with relaxing lavender oil. Your image need not be a static scene. It can change and move, as long as the ambience is one of peace and calm.

Another tried-and-tested method to calm the mind is to recite a *mantra*—a word or phrase that can be recited over and over to calm or focus the mind. In ancient Eastern traditions mantras were believed to be sacred sounds that helped the person chanting them to connect with cosmic forces. Probably the best-known Eastern mantra is the word "Om," but you can use any word or phrase that has meaning for you, for example, "Peace" or "I am calm." The important thing is to pick a mantra that appeals to you intuitively.

Before you start to recite your mantra, make sure that you are sitting comfortably. Close your eyes and slow down your breathing. Then start to chant your mantra rhythmically, so that the sounds resonate, washing away any anxiety and replacing it with total peace. Mantras are usually most effective when recited slowly, but try varying the pace and your intonation until you arrive at the best combination—you will know instinctively when you find this as your chanting will feel effortless.

One of the biggest problems we encounter when we try to relax the mind and silence mental chatter is that we keep getting distracted. Don't worry if this happens to you—it is perfectly normal. The trick is to acknowledge any thoughts that creep in and then just let them go. Tell yourself that you will deal with them later—you could even keep a notebook to hand to write down anything important. Then, gently refocus on your visualization or mantra and continue to relax your mind.

When you are a beginner at relaxing your mind, tranquil surroundings can sometimes help you to succeed. However, an oasis of calm is not easy to find in a noisy, bustling city. If you can't find a quiet corner at home, why not try one of the city's parks? You can often find an empty bench set away from the main pathways, where you can sit surrounded by trees and plants. And don't forget places of worship. Even if you are not religious, you can always visit a church or a synagogue to sit quietly for a few minutes in peaceful contemplation.

Making Your Life Simpler

Life can get complicated. And if you live in a city, your life can get very complicated very quickly, because city life is faster and at times almost chaotic. In a city, finding enough living space is always a problem—you often don't have enough room for all your accumulated "stuff." And city life is expensive. You notice, painfully, that you never have enough money to live in the style you would like. And at some point you question why you are living this hurried, more acquisitive, more complicated lifestyle.

This chapter shows you how to simplify your life in the city. You will discover how to live in the present and appreciate the here-and-now. You will see how to be better organized and reduce your clutter, as well as how to manage your time so you can do the things you feel are important. And you will find out how to handle your money more wisely. In short, you will learn how to eliminate what you do not need, and be happier with less.

Taking a Stroll in the Fast Lane

Probably the most common source of discontent for people who live in the city is the hectic pace of life. City living can be fast, and at times even furious. It seems that we urbanites suffer from "hurry sickness"—trying to do too much in too short a period of time. We walk too fast, we talk too fast, we eat too fast, we do just about everything too fast. When we rush, our minds race and we feel anxious to accomplish whatever we are rushing to do. If we can't keep up our hectic pace, we become more anxious, more worried. Our bodies become tense, our immune systems come under pressure and we are vulnerable to illness—at some point, our minds and bodies pay the price.

Why we hurry so much is not that difficult to figure out. Our culture and society give importance to "doing" rather than simply "being." We value accomplishment and success. The notion of slowing down, of doing less and accomplishing less, seems at variance with what we *think* we should be doing. We rush, often not knowing why. We lose track of time; hours turn into days, weeks turn into months, even years. At some point, when we are forced to slow down—say, by illness—and have time for reflection, we ask ourselves why we didn't make time simply to enjoy all the wonderful things that life in the city can offer.

LIVE IN THE PRESENT

We race through much of our day, often unaware of what we are doing and what it feels like to be doing it. Living on "auto-pilot" in this way robs us of the satisfaction that comes with really experiencing life. By doing the following exercise we can learn how to become mindful and appreciate each moment. You will need a pen and paper.

1. Start by becoming more aware of how much you rush around. Make an effort to notice when you hurry most. For example, do you really rush in the morning, taking a shower, getting dressed, and even driving to work without any recollection of having done these things afterward? Keep a "Hurry Log" for a week, noting down times and situations in which you are particularly prone to losing touch with the present.

2. Study your Hurry Log to see if you can discern a pattern in your hurrying behavior. Resolve to make an extra effort at those times and in those situations that you have recorded in your log.

3. Next, take a close look at how you carry out your daily routine, especially chores and everyday tasks—too often we do these with little awareness and enjoyment. Choose one activity, such as doing your laundry or washing the dishes, and make a point of doing it mindfully each day for a week. It may help to give a running commentary to yourself, describing each action as you carry it out.

4. One by one increase the number of tasks that you do mindfully each day.

As well as the hectic pace of city life, upsetting ourselves about the past, or worrying about what might happen in the future are also sources of stress. With one foot in the past, and the other in the future, we miss the present. This is unfortunate, because if we could learn to be "mindful"—to focus on what is happening right at this moment—our lives could be less stressful and more fulfilling. Once you live in the present, you also find that the time passes much less quickly, providing an important antidote to the frantic pace of life.

You might think that slowing yourself down and living in the moment would be fairly easy. But knowing that you *should* slow down, and *actually* slowing down are two different things. And, like most people, you probably find it hard to stay in the present. The past and the future are like magnets pulling your attention away from what you are doing at the moment. Slowing down your lifestyle and living in the present may be behaviors that you need to learn. And just as with other skills, they take time, effort, and practice to acquire. So persevere, because the results are well worth it. You will find that there is far less stress in your life and far more satisfaction. More often than you might think, it's better to take a stroll in the fast lane.

EXERCISE 8

EAT MINDFULLY

For many of us who live in the city, eating is something we do in great haste. Learning to eat mindfully can help you to rediscover the sensual pleasure of eating and is another important step in learning to slow down in the city.

1. When you have your next meal, instead of starting to eat straight away, take a few moments to have a good look at your food. Feast your eyes on the different colors, shapes, and textures. Appreciate the way it has been arranged on the plate.

2. Next, close your eyes and notice the various aromas emanating from your food. Can you identify the dominant smells? What ingredients can you recognize from their pungency alone?

3. Now, really taste your food. Savor each bite. Notice the way that the food feels in your mouth. Think about all the different flavors you can taste, as you chew it slowly and for much longer than you would normally.

4. When you are about halfway through your food, pause for a few moments. Then, as you start to eat again, look at the food before you put it in your mouth. Notice the aftertaste from this bite and anticipate the taste of the next. Savor the flavors.

5. Continue to eat your whole meal in this focused way. Once you are able to pay more attention to what you are eating, expand your mindfulness to take in your place setting, the tableware, and your surroundings.

Winning the Waiting Game

Waiting, unfortunately, is a part of life. And if you live in a city, you will definitely have to wait. You will wait in traffic, wait for your bus or train to arrive, and wait for your elevator. You will find yourself waiting for your doctor or dentist who, more often than not, will be running late. You will wait in line at the movie theater, the bank, and the supermarket, and for the person on the other end of the 'phone line to take you off hold. Rarely a day goes by in which, at some point, you don't find yourself having to wait for someone or something. You can either let the waiting get to you or you can win the waiting game. You just need to know how to play.

First, master the art of "off-peaking." This means doing what you have to do at a time when few other people are doing it. Take your banking, for example. You could go to your bank at lunchtime on a Friday and wait with everyone else. Or you could make things less stressful by going at an off-peak time on a less busy day. The first and last days of the month are the busiest times in banks, so try to avoid these. Use the automated cash dispensers whenever possible. Pay your bills by mail. Better still, if you have a computer, do your banking transactions on-line.

Similarly, try to make appointments with your doctor and your dentist for less busy times. Obviously, this depends on how flexible you schedule is, but a good time for such appointments is mid- to late morning, or directly after lunch, preferably mid-week. Mondays and Fridays are always busy, as there are extra people who need treatment after the weekend, or who need last-minute appointments before the weekend. The off-peak advantage also applies to gyms and health clubs. Again, Mondays can be very busy, as people rush to work out when they feel guilty about having over-indulged over the weekend. Later in the week the numbers drop off. Lunchtime is more popular, but not as bad as after 5.30pm. Week-day mornings and afternoons can be a much less crowded time to work out, if you can find the time.

Even the leisure industries keep us waiting these days. How often have you had to wait in line for a table at a restaurant? If you are going out for lunch or dinner, try to eat either a little later or a little earlier than the mob. Off-peak, the service is better, the atmosphere is more relaxed, and you get a better table. And if you like to see plays or go to the movies, avoid waiting by buying your tickets in advance over the 'phone or on-line. Then, simply pick up your tickets when you arrive at the theater or movie theater. There may be a small charge for this service, but the savings in terms of time and energy are well worth it.

Other ways to cut waiting times include 'phoning through your grocery order to your local supermarket so that they deliver it—thereby saving you the hassle of waiting in line at the checkout. You might also be able to 'phone or fax your medical prescriptions to your local drugstore, or even have your doctor call in the prescription. In most larger cities many things can be done at night, after office closing times. There are all-night drugstores, supermarkets, bookstores, videostores, and just about everything else you might need. And don't forget your computer. With a few well-placed taps on your keyboard and clicks of your mouse you can summon up any one of thousands of websites. These days going on-line offers access to most goods and services.

When you do find yourself having to wait, use the time productively, entertainingly, or at least pleasantly. Keep some reading material with you whenever you go out, or carry a personal stereo or CD player so that you can listen to music. Then again, you could try to relax (see exercise, opposite). Waiting time is also useful for catching up on any organizing or planning. For example, you could put together a shopping list, or update your To-Do list, or make notes about an upcoming event or trip. Just be sure always to keep a pen and a notepad to hand.

PRACTICE RAPID RELAXATION

The ability to relax when you are under pressure in the city can make a significant contribution to your well-being. Try this simple relaxation technique when you are stuck in a line, sitting in a traffic jam, or whenever you find yourself having to wait.

1. Inhale fully through your nostrils, filling your lungs right to the bottom. At the same time squeeze your right thumb and index finger together. Hold the squeeze and your breath for 7 or 8 seconds.

2. Exhale fully and slowly through slightly parted lips while releasing any tension in your right hand and arm. At the same time, imagine a wave of relaxation flowing from the top of your head down through your body all the way to your toes.

3. Next, inhale again through your nostrils, but this time squeeze your left thumb and index finger together. Again, hold the squeeze and your breath for 7 or 8 seconds.

4. Now spend a few moments breathing slowly and deeply, making sure that you are using your diaphragm muscles (see p.26).

5. Repeat this exercise whenever the opportunity arises—it will help you to relax your whole body fairly quickly and slow any build-up of muscle tension.

Managing Your Time

When you live in a city, you quickly recognize that there really is never enough time to do everything that you would like to do. You find that you have more things to do, and less time in which to do them. Your life becomes unpredictable, and it seems to be the city, and not you, that sets your agenda. Unless you begin managing your own life, you realize that the city will manage it for you.

Effective time-management does not mean trying to do everything in the least amount of time. Doing it all is impossible, not to mention incredibly stressful. Managing your time effectively means managing your priorities. Not all the things you have to do have the same importance or value. You may find yourself spending your time doing things that don't turn out to be worthwhile. One of the secrets of effective time management is knowing what's important to you and then figuring out ways of spending more of your time doing those important things.

One of the big advantages of living in a city is the large number of errands that can be accomplished without having to leave your home. There is very little that cannot be delivered to your door—groceries, laundry, clothes, just about anything. And as you live in restaurant heaven, take advantage of the easy access to all manner of prepared food at all manner of hours, and order in.

USE THE "WILL-DO" APPROACH

Most of us simply do not plan our days carefully enough, and so we make ourselves more vulnerable to the stresses of urban life. Try using the "will-do"
approach to minimize these stresses and to improve how you organize your day.
You will need a notebook and a pen for this exercise.

*1. Open your notebook and at the top of the first page write today's date (or if you
are making your list in the evening, tomorrow's date). Underneath this, draw 3
columns and from left to right label them "Will Do," "When and Where," and
"The Outcome.".*

*2. In the first column, under "Will Do," jot down the things that you wish to
accomplish today. These are the tasks that will cause you stress if you don't do them.
The list can be long or short, but write down only those tasks that have high priority or
importance in your life, because you are committing yourself to do them. Then, fill in
the details in the "When and Where" column. You are now ready to do all those things
on your "Will Do" list.*

*3. Toward the end of the day, give yourself 10 minutes in which to write up your results
under "The Outcome." Take a moment to pat yourself on the back and revel in the
satisfaction of all that you have achieved. Then, on a new page, draw up 3 more
columns and repeat the process, listing what you hope to get done tomorrow. (If for
any reason something didn't get done today, and it is still important, put it at the top of
tomorrow's list.)*

Often, making your life simpler, less stressful, and giving yourself more time to do the things you like to do entails paying someone else to do the things that you hate to do, or do not do very well, and/or do not have the time to do. Realistically assess your financial ability to hire someone, say, to clean your home once a week. The extra time you gain will be well worth the money.

Constant interruptions and distractions from what you need to get done, both at work and at home, are another time-wasting facet of city life. One good way to avoid being interrupted is to switch on your voicemail. Then, you won't have to fend off people who want to persuade you to switch your long-distance courier or to sell you cheaper insurance. Even better, install caller ID, so that you can screen your calls and answer only the important ones. And even if you do not have voicemail, you don't have to answer the 'phone every time it rings. If someone really needs to speak with you, they will keep trying until they reach you.

And did I mention time spent watching television? Yes, there are many worthwhile programs to watch, but often we waste time in front of the TV when we could be doing something much more interesting or useful. So, cut back your viewing and instead read a book, bake a cake, or spend more time with your kids.

LEARN TO DELEGATE

To ensure that you make the most effective use of your time, you need to be able to delegate. This is not always as straightforward as it sounds, particularly if you are a perfectionist. Try this exercise, which will help you to become less anxious about trusting others to do a good job.

1. *Whether it's asking someone to write an important report for you at work or to clean your kitchen, find the right person for the job. Make sure that the person to whom you are delegating has the experience, knowledge, and skills to do the task asked of them. And if you can't find anyone who has the know-how, consider having someone trained or showing them how to do it yourself.*

2. *Be sure to ask for help in a positive way. Tell the person why you selected him or her. Offer a genuine compliment reflecting that you recognize some ability or competence that makes that person right for the job. Be appreciative of their time. Recognize that you're aware the person has other work to do, but that you would really be grateful if he or she could help you with this task.*

3. *Once you have assigned the task and carefully explained what needs to be done, let the person do it—don't micro-manage. The person will probably have their own approach and may not do it the same way as you would. But keep your distance unless you see clearly that things are taking a wrong turn. If the person does a good job, say so. And if he or she doesn't do it in quite the way you would have liked, but puts in a lot of effort, let them know that you appreciate their hard work.*

When Less is More

Simplifying your life in the city means ridding yourself of, or at least keeping to a minimum, the "stuff" that you have. Most of us keep too many possessions and paperwork, yet most city housing is less than spacious. As you accumulate things you find that you have less space in which to put them. Gradually, you begin to feel as if the walls are closing in on you. And when you live a busy, city lifestyle, it is often difficult to find the time to sort out and get rid of all your excess "stuff."

When you do finally get around to a clutter-bust, you discover that you are are strangely resistant to getting rid of things. Somehow, actually parting with "stuff" is much harder than you'd anticipated. Deep-down we believe that we really *will* clean out that closet, donate those old clothes to charity, or pass on all our hand-me-downs. We also kid ourselves that we will eventually use all the things that we haven't used in eons, that anything that has even a whiff of sentimental value must be kept no matter what, and that if something is worth even a few dollars, it must be worth keeping—forever. So, how can you break this hold that your things seem to have over you?

First, schedule in some time to deal with your clutter. When we schedule events they have a better chance of getting done—we generally show up at medical appointments and business meetings. So, set aside a definite time for tackling your clutter and write it down in your calendar.

Jump-start your organizational drive by using the technique that I call "salami-slicing." Rather than seeing all your extra stuff as one large mass of clutter, divide it into groups that can be tackled one at a time, piece by piece, slice by slice.

Start with things that are relatively self-contained. For example, if you feel snowed under with household paperwork, sort it out into categories, such as bank statements, mortgage or rent, utility bills, insurance, and so on, and file it. Keep only what you *really* need—for example, important documents. You may want to keep an article, a recipe, a travel brochure, a warranty, an instruction manual, a medical record, or that receipt you will need for your tax return. Fine. Put it into an appropriately labeled file and then put the file away. But, try to be ruthless and get rid of any unimportant paperwork that is, say, more than a year old.

Once you have conquered the paperwork, move on to another type of clutter, such as old clothes. In this way you can gradually liberate yourself from unwanted clutter until your entire home is as neat as you would like it to be.

Simplifying your lifespace takes determination. If you find yourself wavering, try asking yourself questions such as: "Do I really want to spend the next twenty years living with this?"and "If my place were on fire and I could save only half of what I own, would I save this particular item?" If you still can't make a decision, see the exercise opposite for how to apply my own technique for effective clutter-busting.

You could also try getting a "clutter buddy." Whenever my wife and I decide to have a purge on clutter, we find that we are each good at clearing out the other person's stuff. So invite your partner or a friend to guide you as to what things should go and what should stay. Of course, you can then return the favor.

If it helps, make a list of rewards that could motivate you to tackle your clutter. Then, give yourself a treat, such as a special meal or a trip to the movies, each time you succeed. Whatever you choose, make it *fun*—you've earned it.

Bear in mind that your goal is not magazine-perfect rooms, minimalist chic, or a spartan lifespace. Some degree of clutter and disorganization can be satisfying and emotionally comforting. It is the unwanted and distressing clutter that needs to be eliminated. Don't defoliate. Prune.

MINIMIZE YOUR CLUTTER

One of the biggest obstacles to getting rid of things is having to make that one all-important decision: "Should I keep it, or should I get rid of it?" One trick I have found useful in overcoming this dilemma is to use something I call the "Triage Method of Clutter Control." Here's how it works.

1. Decide which clutter you are going to clear out first. You could tackle it by type—for example, books, ornaments, and so on; or you could do it room by room, starting with most cluttered room first.

2. Sort out your clutter into three separate piles: "Definitely Keep," "Not Sure," and "Definitely Get Rid Of." Your attitude should be "I'm sick and tired of having all this stuff and I'm going to get rid of as much as I can." This means that you will have to be tough with yourself.

3. Throw out or give away everything in the "Definitely Get Rid Of" and "Not Sure" piles. Don't hesitate—just steel yourself and do it. If you feel guilty about throwing away perfectly good things, quickly organize a yard sale or donate them to a charity, such as the Salvation Army or a local community organization. (But make sure that you set yourself a firm timeframe within which you must get rid of them or you will defeat your objective of clutter-busting.)

4. Resolve to keep on top of your clutter and set a date for another clear-out in 6 months' time.

The Art of Low-cost Living

There's no doubt about it, living in a city can be very expensive. Simple economic principles dictate that where there is high demand and limited supply, everything costs more. Housing (owning or renting), clothing, transport, food, and entertainment can all cost a bundle.

The fact is, above a certain salary-level, there is no strong correlation between your income and your financial woes. The amount of fiscal distress you experience comes largely from the difference between what you can *afford* to spend and what you *do* spend. In the final analysis, managing money in the city comes down to managing your priorities.

If your mortgage or rent is very high, try taking in a lodger or finding someone to move in with you and share the rent. You can save the extra money for a proverbial rainy day or use it to enjoy yourself. And just because you live in a city doesn't mean that you must always deck yourself out in the latest designer wear. If you like to be fashionable and have expensive tastes, limit yourself to one "must-have" item each season and shop around to get the latest look from cheaper stores. Or, if being up to date is not a priority but wearing good-quality clothing is, shop only in the sales when you can make big savings (provided that you are

EXERCISE 13

TRACK YOUR EXPENDITURE

It is easy to fritter away money when you live in the city. By getting you to record what you spend every day for a month, this exercise will give you an overview of where your money goes, so that you can take steps to curb your spending. You will need a pen and a notebook.

1. Write today's date at the top of the first page in your notebook. You are going to carry this around with you each day for a month and make a note of every expenditure, whether by cash, debit card, or credit card. (If this seems impractical, keep all your receipts and then enter details of your spending in your notebook when you have a spare moment during the day.) Make sure that you record every amount, no matter how small, and include a brief description next to it, for example "$5.60 (magazine)."

2. At the end of the month, divide your spending into columns according to types of expenditure, such as Transportation, Groceries, Rent/Mortgage, Eating Out, and so on. Then, add up how much you have spent under each heading.

3. Now analyze the totals. Putting aside fixed payments, such as your rent or mortgage, and any one-off expenditures, such as servicing your car, is there any total that seems shockingly high? For example, did you spend rather a lot on eating out? List any key areas where you could cut your spending, and resolve to spend less.

4. Repeat this exercise in a couple of months' time to monitor how effective you have been at reducing your expenditure in the key area(s) you identified above.

disciplined and don't get carried away and buy things you will never wear, just because they have a fifty-per cent discount.)

Transportation is probably one of your bigger expenditures. Living in the city, running a car can be prohibitively expensive—parking and gas are usually more costly and insurance premiums are usually higher than elsewhere. It has been estimated that you can save up to $100 a month if you leave your car at home and use public transportation. Even better, walk—especially in the summer. If you're going to buy a car, consider getting a used one. If you absolutely must have that new-car smell, buy last year's model just after the new replacements come out.

Eating out is an intrinsic part of life in the city. And you can do it without breaking the bank. Every city has many great places to eat, and not all of them are expensive. The best places are often recommended by word of mouth, but a good starting point would be a comprehensive, up-to-date restaurant guide.

Every city offers an array of free or low-cost cultural events, such as concerts, opera, dance, musicals, and plays. Sometimes these are staged at lunchtime, but often they are in the evenings and at weekends. Check with the city's cultural events office or access their website for details.

SHOP, DON'T BUY!

The temptation to buy can run high if you live in the city—there is no shortage of things to spend your money on. But just because there is something you'd *like* to buy it does not mean that you *have* to buy it. This exercise will help you learn to think twice before getting out your wallet.

1. When it comes to shopping, there is a big difference between looking and actually buying. The next time you are tempted to buy something costing over say, $20, give yourself time to consider the purchase before rushing to spend the money. By all means have a close look at the item, handle it, or try it on if that's appropriate, but whatever you do—don't buy it.

2. As you look at the item, ask yourself the following questions: "Do I really need this?" "Will this item truly add to the quality of my life?" "Can I really afford to buy it?" If you answer "no" to any of these questions, it is obvious that you shouldn't buy the item. If you answer "yes" to all three, tell yourself that you'll come back and buy it tomorrow —then leave the store.

3. Consider the potential purchase overnight, and if you are still keen to purchase it the next day, then go ahead. But, curiously, you will often find that your enthusiasm has waned, or even evaporated by the next day.

4. Apply this technique to any potential purchases over $20, thereby indulging your desire to shop; but curbing your impulse to buy.

Becoming More Resilient

Think Stressed, Be Stressed

Your Thinking Errors

Anger and You

Tempering Your Temper

Worrying Less

Developing Inner Confidence

Knowing What's Important

Finding Your Spiritual Side

By this point, you have acquired a number of tools that will help you cope with city life. You have learned how to relax your body, and quieten your mind. You have discovered ways of simplifying your life and slowing it down. But there is more. You also need to learn how to strengthen your inner resources. You need to become resilient from within.

This chapter will help you develop your emotional muscle and become psychologically stronger. It will teach you how to recognize and, ultimately, change the ways in which you think and look at the world. To do this you will have to learn how to assess and, at times, change your beliefs, attitudes, and values. You will find out which of those beliefs, attitudes, and values contribute to or reduce your stress. In short, you will discover how to turn your stress-*producing* thinking into stress-*resistant* thinking so that you become more resilient to city life.

Think Stressed, Be Stressed

Have you ever noticed how people react differently to exactly the same situation? If you take a random group and expose them to the same stress or hassle in the city, the chances are that you will get a range of reactions. What is stressful for one person may be less stressful or not stressful at all for you. How come?

Most people tend to think of stress as something that is external—caused by an event, a situation, or a person. And to some extent this is true. However, you play a more important role in creating your own stress than you might have imagined. Feeling stressed is, and always has been, a two-part process. There has to be a trigger (something that sets off your stress), but there also has to be something within you that reacts to that trigger.

By changing the way you think about a potentially stressful situation, you can change the way you react emotionally to that situation. It is perfectly possible to feel very stressed because you think about something in one way; but if you can think about it in another way you can feel less stressed, or maybe not stressed at all.

The following exercise will help you to assess the degree to which your way of thinking plays a role in exacerbating your stress levels. The next few pages will show you specific ways of recognizing and changing stress-inducing ways of thinking.

FIND YOUR BALANCE

This exercise will help you to determine the extent to which your faulty thinking plays a part in making you stressed. You will need a pen and some paper.

1. Think of an event, a situation, or a person that recently caused you stress. Now, rate the level of stress you felt, using a scale of 1 to 10, where 1 = not stressed at all, and 10 = extremely stressed. ("Stress" here can mean any type of distress or emotion—anger, upset, annoyance, sadness, disappointment, frustration, worry, and so on.)

2. Next, rate the relative importance of your stress. Using a similar scale to the one used in step 1 above, rate the relative importance of the trigger—the event, the situation, or the person that caused your stress. To help you get the scale in proportion, think of 9s and 10s as the major life-altering events, such as the death of a loved one or severe financial problems; and think of 1s and 2s as minor annoyances, such as missing your bus or mislaying your keys.

3. Now compare the two by asking yourself: "Does the stress I am feeling match the importance of the situation?" If, for example, your stress level is a 7, and the importance of the situation is a 3, you are getting quite stressed over something that doesn't warrant it—you are overreacting and contributing to much of your own stress.

4. Do this exercise to rate your reaction whenever you suspect that you might have gotten things out of proportion. Then, see pp.58–61 for advice on how to change your faulty thinking.

Your Thinking Errors

If you wish to be able to regain and maintain your emotional balance, you need to know how to change your way of thinking. This entails being able to identify your thinking errors and distortions, and then to correct them.

Let's look at some of the most common. If, on finding yourself stuck in a traffic jam, you say to yourself, "Oh my gosh, this is a catastrophe! This is awful!", you are guilty of "catastrophizing" and "awfulizing"—turning an everyday hassle into a major tragedy, which elevates your stress levels. To feel less stressed teach yourself to put things in perspective. Ask yourself, "How important is this *really*?" "Will I remember this incident in three months, three weeks, or even three days?" The chances are that you will have forgotten about it by tomorrow.

Next is "can't-stand-this-itis," a form of emotional distortion. It occurs in a situation you do not like, when you overreact and say to yourself "I can't stand this!", so that you become far more upset than is warranted by the situation. As soon as you think "I can't stand this!", you need to check yourself and consider honestly whether you are exaggerating the way you feel.

Or, perhaps you are guilty of "overgeneralizing." Do you ever think, "I always have to do everything myself," (when, say,

LEARN TO THINK POSITIVELY

Everyone experiences setbacks from time to time—they are an inescapable part of life. But how we let adversity affect us depends on our attitude toward it. This exercise will help you discover—and change—the negative thinking patterns that make your life in the city stressful.

1. Sit somewhere comfortable and close your eyes. Think of a recent time when you found yourself in a difficult or adverse situation. It could be anything from missing your flight to having your purse stolen or being overlooked for promotion at work. Take a few moments to recall the emotions you felt at the time.

2. Next, with the benefit of hindsight, ask yourself how you could have made the situation less stressful if you had changed the way you thought about it at the time. For example, could you have just accepted it as something beyond your control, and moved on? Or, could you have acknowledged your feelings, and thought about how to make the best of a bad situation? Or then again, could you have told yourself it would soon be over and before long you would be home, safe and sound? Consider the thinking strategy that would have worked best for you at the time.

3. Now revisit the original situation, but this time imagine yourself applying the thinking strategy that you chose in step 2. You should feel much less stressed about it this time. Keep your chosen thinking strategy in mind so that you can implement it whenever you are faced with a setback.

your request for a family member to take out the trash goes unanswered.) When you overgeneralize you create a distorted image of what is really happening by thinking in an all-or-nothing way, making yourself more stressed than you need to be. Look out for language that reflects this extreme thinking—words like "always" and "never" and replace them with "sometimes" to diffuse stress.

You "mind-read" and "conclusion-jump" whenever you believe something to be true, when, in fact, it may not be true at all. For example, say you don't receive an invitation to a friend's party, so you conclude that they must dislike you. Instead, you need to ask yourself, "Do I really have enough evidence to support this belief?" If the answer is no, tell yourself that you are being at best irrational, and at worst, paranoid. There could be a simple explanation, such as that the invitation went missing in the post.

Whenever you "what-if", you fantasize that a situation or event that *could* happen, probably *will* happen. For example, when the apartment above is sold you immediately start panicking about how you will cope with the noise if the new owners are avid musicians. Ask yourself: "Realistically, what are the chances of this really happening?" and "When I'm old and I reflect back on my life, will this seem important?" Probably not.

COUNT YOUR BLESSINGS

There is no doubt that the pressures of city life can cause us to get stressed by relatively petty things. Sometimes it can help to pause and take stock of all the good things we have in our lives. This exercise will help you to put your anxieties in perspective.

1. Start by thinking about yourself. Consider your health and ask yourself the following questions: Am I able to walk? Can I speak, hear, see? Tell yourself how lucky you are to have an able body and a sound mind.

2. Next think about the people you share your life with—your partner, parents, siblings, children, friends, and colleagues. Take a moment to think about the people who mean most to you. Tell yourself how lucky you are to have such wonderful people around you.

3. Now consider your circumstances. Do you have somewhere to live? Do you have enough food to eat? Do you have enough money to pay your way? Tell yourself how lucky you are to be able to live without hardship.

4. Finally, turn your thoughts to the things you really enjoy. Do you go regularly to the theater or the movies? Do you eat out at restaurants? Do you visit art galleries and museums? Do you go for walks in the park? Tell yourself how lucky you are to have so many opportunities to enjoy the pleasures of city life.

Anger and You

If you live in a city, there is no shortage of potential situations ready to trigger your anger. We all feel angry at some time or other, but unfortunately, too many of us experience too much anger too much of the time.

Getting angry is not without consequences because it can increase levels of important stress hormones, such as epinephrine (adrenaline) and cortisol, which can have negative physical effect on the heart and cardiovascular system. Angry individuals also typically engage in a number of behaviors that can have bad effects on their bodies, such as smoking, drinking, and overeating.

Hostility and aggression, which are both types of anger, can be very destructive to interpersonal relationships. Your anger affects the people you live with, work with, and interact with—your partner, children, friends, and co-workers, and it can lead to conflict, mental and physical abuse, breakups, and divorce.

Does this mean that all anger is inappropriate or destructive? No, not at all. In fact, in measured doses and when expressed in the right ways, anger can be an appropriate and effective emotion. It can motivate you to take action to resolve the situation that triggered your anger in the first place. Try the exercise opposite to find out your own anger levels.

DETERMINE YOUR ANGER LEVELS

Read the following statements, and then indicate the extent to which each describes you. Give yourself 3 points if the statement "strongly" describes you; 2 points if it "somewhat" describes you; and 1 point if it doesn't describe you at all. Then add up your score. You will need a pen and some paper.

1. *I feel that my anger is excessive.*
2. *My anger has frequently gotten me into trouble in the past.*
3. *My family and friends tell me I get angry too easily.*
4. *I hold on to my anger longer than I should.*
5. *I get frustrated pretty easily.*
6. *Petty annoyances can make me fly off the handle.*
7. *I hate waiting or being kept waiting.*
8. *I get angry when traffic or lines don't move fast enough.*
9. *Incompetence and stupidity in others makes me angry.*
10. *I take criticism and disapproval badly.*
11. *Being treated rudely or unfairly makes me very angry.*
12. *In arguments, I'm usually the one who usually gets the most angry.*

Your score

Less than 18 points: you do not have a problem with anger.

Between 19 and 30 points: anger affects your life moderately.

Between 31 to 36 points: you need to take steps to reduce your anger levels.

Tempering Your Temper

Anger is not an automatic reaction beyond your control, even though at times it may feel like that. Rather, it is a response that you can control to a large extent.

One of the most important things you can do to control anger is to learn how to talk yourself out of it. When confronted with a difficult situation, you can either say things to yourself that stoke your anger, or say things that reduce or even eliminate it. In using self-talk in this way, you have a powerful tool that can help you to keep your temper in check.

To follow are some useful examples of anger-reducing self-talk that might work for you. Choose the ones that best fit your situation, or think up some effective ones of your own.

• Is this really worth getting angry about?

• I don't have to feel angry about this if I choose not to.

• Getting angry is not going to improve the situation.

• I won't take the bait.

• I'll stay cool; I'll stay calm.

• I'll take a deep breath and count to ten.

• I'll let this go—it's not worth the emotional stress.

• I won't take this personally.

• I must remember that everyone sees things differently.

- I must accept that other people have different priorities.
- I must accept that people have the right to be wrong.
- I mustn't judge the person, just their behavior.
- Do I think that this is really such a big deal?
- Will I recall this in three years? Three months, weeks, days, even hours?

There are probably times when you become angry because you are caught off-guard and you react emotionally, before your head can evaluate the situation in a more rational way. One effective strategy for combating this emotional response is to begin to anticipate which situations and circumstances usually trigger your anger, and plan ahead so that you can handle them without getting angry. Before the situation occurs, rehearse what you are going to say and how you want to feel. You can usually identify upcoming situations in which you know that your chances of getting angry are high. One such situation may be when you're about to discuss something with someone, and you know that they will be less than receptive or even downright opposed to what you have to say. This could be when you have to deal with a client or a co-worker, a relative or a friend, or even a sales clerk in a store at the local shopping mall.

Once you have anticipated a potential anger-producing situation in advance, the next step is to imagine it happening. Let's assume that you have a meeting scheduled with your boss to discuss how to handle a difficult client and you have very different approaches. Visualize the meeting in as much detail as possible. For example, if you know that the potential confrontation will take place in your boss's office, conjure up the setting as vividly as you can, right down to the picture of their spouse and kids they keep on their desk. Then imagine your boss sitting at their desk in their habitual way. See yourself confidently entering their office and sitting down opposite them in a purposeful but relaxed way. Next, envisage what you will say and how you will act. Your goal, of course, is to control your anger levels. Imagine that your boss disagrees completely with what you propose. You can see them starting to get angry and you start to feel your anger building in response. Now, imagine using self-talk to calm yourself down and to stop yourself going for the bait. Watch yourself as you keep your anger level low. Notice how calm and in control you feel. Rehearse in this way several times in your head before the meeting. Chances are, when the situation does occur, you will handle it much better than you would have done in the past.

LOOK ON THE FUNNY SIDE

Humor can be an important tool in helping you to diffuse anger. If you can find something about a situation that makes you laugh, or at least brings a smile to your face, your anger will evaporate. Try this exercise whenever you find your patience wearing thin.

1. Imagine that you are on the bus on your way to work, when you find yourself stuck in an incredibly long traffic jam that stretches as far as the eye can see, both ahead and behind your vehicle. The traffic is hardly moving at all.

2. While you are waiting you call your office and various members of your family and friends on your cell phone; you try to read your newspaper or book; you listen to music on your CD player, but you can't really concentrate. Your fellow passengers are also restless and some are starting to get agitated. You feel yourself gradually getting frustrated and becoming angry.

3. Now use your imagination to turn this potentially unpleasant scenario into a funny one. Exaggerate the situation in your mind by visualizing that you are going to be stuck on the bus for days. Imagine your boss emailing you work via your laptop. Picture your family coming to visit you, bringing food. You develop strong friendships with some of the other passengers. There is talk of taking vacations together and of reunions. Let your imagination run riot—the more absurd you can make the situation in your mind, the easier it will be to diffuse your anger.

Worrying Less

It may be because of the fast pace or pressures of city life, but many urbanites are worriers. As well worrying about the big issues in life such as work, relationships, children, health, and finances, we also worry about the little things, such as whether or not we can get across town in time for a meeting or whether or not we can get a table at our favorite restaurant. The result is a never-ending succession of stressful situations which can sometimes build up and make us feel overwhelmed.

So just how do you get this worrying under control? Simply telling yourself to stop does little good—you need some tools to help you. Start by using your coping self-talk (see pp.64–5). Talk to yourself in ways that will help you to look at things differently. Here are some examples of self-statements and questions that you can use to help you to deal with situations that make you feel anxious:

• I mustn't make this a bigger deal than it really is.
• How likely is it that my worst-case scenario is going to happen?
• I mustn't assume the worst will happen. Most often it doesn't!
• Is there another, more sensible way, of looking at this?
• How would a good friend or a role model approach the problem?
• I can cope with this.

- Take a nice deep breath. Hold it. And let it all out slowly.
- Realistically, what is the worst that can happen?
- Is worrying helping me in any way?
- What can I do to distract myself from these anxieties?
- Stop what-if-ing!
- On a scale of zero to ten, how important is this really?

Doing some exercise is an excellent way to take you away from your worries—try worrying while you are jogging, rowing, swimming, lifting weights, climbing, hitting a golf or tennis ball, or doing any other form of exercise or sport. It's not easy. If exercise per se is not your thing, just go for a walk. A brisk walk is even more effective. When you are walking, you are distracted, and you are releasing physical stress and tension—all terrific antidotes to stress.

Writing down your anxieties can help you to worry less. Much of your worrying goes on in a vague, ill-defined way. Sometimes even you aren't quite sure what you're so concerned about. By writing down your anxieties, you begin to feel that you are more in control of them. You don't have to write volumes. One study found that when the participants wrote down their concerns for only twenty minutes per day over three consecutive days, approximately half of them experienced positive effects that seemed to last for months.

Another good anti-worrying tactic is to distract yourself by keeping busy—it is difficult to worry about something while you're concentrating on something else. You could watch TV, read a good book, go shopping, or do some cooking, gardening or carpentry. In fact, you could involve yourself in any activity that can hold your attention and take you away from your anxieties.

One useful, albeit strange-sounding, strategy is to do your worrying at designated times each day. Call this your "worry time." When you sense that anxieties are creeping into your mind, remind yourself that it is not yet time to think about them and they will have to wait. Start with twenty minutes of worry time. It could be during a coffee break, or after lunch, or on your trip home after work. If you find that twenty minutes is too long, cut back by five minutes each day until you find your optimal time.

And don't forget the value of confiding in another person, such as a family member, a close friend, or simply an understanding and sympathetic listener. We feel better, and worry less, when we've had an opportunity to talk through the things that are bothering us and get our worries in perspective.

ARE YOU A WORRIER?

To help determine whether or not you are worrying too much, simply indicate to what extent each of the 10 statements below applies to you. Use the response categories: "not at all like me," "a little like me," or "a lot like me." You will need a pen and a sheet of paper.

1. Worrying is a major source of stress in my life.

2. After I start worrying, I find it very difficult to stop.

3. People who know me well tell me that I worry too much.

4. I have trouble getting to sleep or falling back to sleep because of my worrying.

5. I often think of worst-case scenarios when I worry about a problem.

6. I frequently worry about things that could happen but usually don't.

7. I have a great deal of difficulty coping with uncertainty.

8. I worry more than I should about small stuff.

9. When I worry I usually just upset myself more, rather than try to resolve my worry.

10. Sometimes I literally worry myself to the point of sickness.

Your score

Answering more than 2 or 3 of these statements with "a lot like me" suggests that your worrying may be making a large contribution to your overall stress levels.

Developing Inner Confidence

When you feel insecure about yourself, you become vulnerable to the demands and criticism of others. Poor self-esteem can create a host of emotional "buttons" that, when pushed by others, magnify the amount of distress you feel.

One of the best ways to develop inner confidence is to stop "self-rating." You self-rate whenever you equate your self-worth with your performance, your attributes, and/or the approval of others. In all cases, the end result is plenty of unnecessary stress, usually appearing as anxiety and depression. Now I can hear you wondering "What's the matter with that? Don't we all want to do well, have terrific attributes, and the approval of others?" Yes, we do. But self-worth based on achievements, attributes, or getting the approval of others can be fragile. The implication is, should you fail, lose your looks, or be disapproved of, your self-worth will plummet. The reality is that there are many times in life when you will not do as well as you would like, when you will not look as good as you would wish, and you will not get approval from others. By making your worth dependent on any or all of the above, you become vulnerable to unnecessary stress.

We all like and want success and approval; it's when we need it to feel good about ourselves that we get into emotional

MEASURE YOUR SELF-ESTEEM

This exercise will help you to measure your self-esteem. Below are some statements that describe how we feel about ourselves. Simply indicate the extent to which you identify with each statement as either "very much," "a little," or "not at all." You will need a pen and a sheet of paper.

1. *I'm really hard on myself when I make a mistake.*
2. *I find it difficult to express my views and opinions in front of others.*
3. *I constantly compare myself with others.*
4. *I can't take criticism or disapproval lightly.*
5. *I brag too much about my accomplishments.*
6. *I get embarrassed easily.*
7. *I hate being the center of attention.*
8. *I'm too shy.*
9. *I hate losing.*
10. *I'm very competitive.*
11. *I feel most other people are better than me.*
12. *I have to do things perfectly.*

Your score

If your answers are mainly "a little" or "not at all," you have a healthy regard for yourself. We probably all agree with some of the above statements at one time or another, but if you identify "very much" with half or more, you could be suffering from low self-esteem and may benefit from working to build it up (see exercise, p.75).

trouble. A better way is to work toward complete self-acceptance. Understand that you are a complex mixture of strengths and weaknesses, which some people will love and some may not. Accepting your positive attributes as well as your negative ones will give you a high degree of emotional resilience.

To develop inner strength you need to minimize your negative self-talk. You have to learn how not to put yourself down. Giving up this self-rating tendency is not the easiest thing to do. It takes time and effort, but if you persevere you can succeed. To start, ask yourself the following questions: Do I really need to have others' approval to feel good about myself? Do I really have to be better than others to feel good about myself? Am I right to expect myself to be perfect, when I don't expect it of others? Can I rate my total worth as an individual on the basis of one or two attributes or abilities? The answer to each of the above, of course, is a resounding "no." None of the above is truly necessary for you to be happy in life—or to feel good about yourself. Try writing down your self-rating thoughts when they occur and then rebut each one. This will help you to challenge your misguided thinking about yourself and replace your negative judgments with a more self-accepting and appreciative attitude.

BOOST YOUR SELF-CONFIDENCE

The sheer pace of city life can mean that we feel we never have time to do anything properly. This, in turn, can make us lose faith in our own abilities and before we know it our self-esteem has suffered. This visualization exercise can help us to regain our self-confidence.

1. Sit somewhere comfortable and close your eyes. Take deep, slow breaths for a minute and try to empty your mind.

2. Think of something you would like to be really good at. It could be a skill such as painting or singing; it could be a sport such as football or swimming; or it could be a vocation or a profession, such as teaching or business management.

3. Visualize yourself in the front row of an auditorium at an awards ceremony. On the rostrum there is a panel of dignitaries. The audience is packed—your family and friends are sitting a few rows behind you and wave encouragingly.

4. Suddenly you hear the words ... "and the award for (you supply the category) of the year goes to (your name goes here)." Feel the surprise, joy, and elation as you watch yourself go up to the rostrum to receive your prize. Everyone is cheering. Bask in the glory of your achievement and feel proud of yourself.

5. Replay this visualization in your mind whenever the strains of city life get you down and your self-esteem needs a boost.

Knowing What's Important

Your goals and values—what you believe is important in your life
—play an important role in determining how you will cope with
the demands of the city. Just as your thinking plays a vital role in
creating (and relieving) your stress, your values and goals can
increase or reduce the amount of contentment in your life.

What, you may ask, have your values and attitudes got to do
with your level of happiness? Actually, quite a bit. What you
think is important and what you value act together in often subtle
yet crucial ways, either to protect you from unhappiness or to
make your life more stressful. Rarely a day goes by without some
decision, some opinion, or some action being determined, or at
least shaped, by your values and attitudes. Your values in large
part determine your goals, your needs, and your wants. And when
you do not reach these goals, or fulfill these needs and wants, you
feel stressed.

You may not even be aware of holding such values and
attitudes. Yet you do. And either consciously or subconsciously
they guide many of your important decisions—everything from
what you eat to how you vote, from what work you do to how you
spend your time and money. Clarifying your values and attitudes
is a good first step in moving toward developing a stress-resilient

philosophy of life. The greater the congruence between your values and your goals, between your decisions and your actions, the lower your stress levels. Think of your values and attitudes as your road map in life. The better the map, the smaller the chance that you'll make a wrong turn.

So how can you get in touch with your core values? You can start by doing the exercise on page 79. And you can also do what I call the "tombstone test" by asking yourself, "When I am gone, what would I like my tombstone to say about me?" (Assume you have a very large tombstone.) Jot down your answers and keep them, as you may find them very illuminating. Include in your tombstone description the answers to the following specific questions: How would I like people to remember me in life? and What would I have liked to have accomplished in my life? By stepping back and looking at the bigger picture in this way, you are forced to consider what exactly you value as worthwhile and important.

Of course, your values and goals will inevitably change as you go through life and your circumstances alter. The significant people who come into and go out of your life will all have an influence. For example, say you have just become a parent and in the past you have spent a lot of money on luxury vacations each year.

In future you might decide to take cheaper vacations and invest the surplus cash to help finance your son or daughter's education, because with the arrival of your child your values and goals, and hence your priorities and responsibilities, have shifted.

At various points in your life, you may also realize that some of your values and goals no longer reflect what you truly believe in. This could be because you have inherited them from others, such as your parents, your peers, your religion, your teachers; or from the corporation or organization you work for, or the community you live in, without ever having questioned them. For example, you may be climbing the career ladder, but what if deep down you suspect that it's the *wrong* ladder? If this is the case, your career, despite being successful, is also a source of stress and you need to assess what steps you can take to bring it more into line with your values and goals (see exercise, opposite).

It is important to make the effort from time to time to assess the relevance of your values and goals to your current lifestyle, because in so doing you may identify areas of your life that you need to change. Even if you are a creature of habit who tends to resist change, remind yourself that being true to yourself is vital if you are to build up resilience to the stresses of city life.

REASSESS YOUR VALUES AND YOUR GOALS

As your life progresses, it is common to come to the realization that what used to be important to you, no longer is. This exercise helps you to assess the differences between how you are living your life on a day-to-day basis and how you would really like to be living. You will need a pen and some paper.

1. Using the pen and a sheet of paper, divide the page into columns and label them: "Relationships," "Home," "Work," and "Finances." Add any other categories that you feel are relevant. Then, taking each of these areas of your life in turn, briefly describe your life as it is now.

2. Now think about the following scenario. You have been told that you only have 5 years left to live, but you are reassured that you will experience no pain and will be able to carry on a totally normal life until your death. Faced with this news, how would you spend the time that you have left? Jot down your thoughts in the columns underneath your first descriptions, and include any unfulfilled dreams or ambitions.

3. Analyze what you have written. Once you clarify your goals, the first steps you need to take in order to reach them will become obvious. Start now! Above all, keep your goals in mind every day and dare to believe that you will realize them.

Finding Your Spiritual Side

We live in a universe that is both mystifying and, at times, over-whelming, so introducing a spiritual dimension into your life can become an important source of inner peace. Having a belief in something greater than just you and your immediate experience can be a powerful force in helping you to create inner calm and cope with the pressures of city life. Faith in something bigger, something cosmic, can help us come to grips with the unknown and perhaps unknowable.

A number of studies now document the importance of faith in strengthening our ability to flourish. For example, one study found that people whose religious beliefs were a central element in their lives experienced less depression than those in a control group. A second set of research looked at the effects of stress on regular churchgoers compared with non-churchgoers. This found that blood pressure measurements were significantly lower in the committed churchgoers than the non-churchgoers and that those who attended church on a routine basis were much less likely to die of heart attacks than those who went infrequently. Clearly, having a belief offers some emotional and physical benefits.

There is no right way or wrong way to discover a sense of spiritual connectedness. For many, the way may take the form of a

CREATE YOUR OWN RITUAL

Even if you don't belong to a particular religion, to be truly at peace you need to rediscover your spiritual side. Whatever your beliefs, devising your own ritual can be a tremendous help in this quest.

1. Decide what you would like to have at the heart of your ritual. For example, you might like to light a candle, or say a prayer, or even listen to a piece of spiritually uplifting music. Pick something that helps you to connect with your spiritual side.

2. Now consider how to open and close your ritual. Perhaps you'd like to start off with a few moments' contemplation to clear your mind. Or, maybe you would like to wash your hands in a bowl of water to symbolize how you are cleansing yourself of worldly matters to focus on the spiritual. To close your ritual you might wish to blow out your candle or perhaps ring a handbell. Choose whatever actions feel right for you.

3. Next, think about where you can carry out your ritual and how you would like to set the scene. You might choose a room that is bathed in light at certain times of the day; if the weather is good, the garden or roof terrace might be ideal. Or, if you have little space, you might just set aside a corner of your bedroom. Create an ambience— perhaps by burning incense or by playing sacred music, such as Gregorian chant.

4. Put all your chosen elements together. Practice your ritual whenever you need a spiritual lift.

belief in God and involvement in a traditional religious system of beliefs. However, your spirituality may take a different guise. It may be a belief in a more global, more vaguely articulated higher power or higher purpose. Or it may entail taking a more down-to-earth approach and embracing a belief in the human spirit, a sense of community, or nature.

Whatever the form your spiritual beliefs take, growing evidence shows that faith can be a powerful stress-buffer, enhancing your ability to handle life's more serious problems. Faith can help you to cope with illness and it may promote longevity. It can provide meaning and purpose. And subscribing to a belief-system can make it easier to find answers to perplexing and distressing questions about our existence, such as: Why are we here? What is the meaning and purpose of life? and What happens when we die?

Faith can also calm you. It often involves prayer and contemplation, which can quieten your mind and relax your body. Also faith can create a sense of community that often brings people together in a mutually supportive way. Having others to be with and share with can make you feel more content. It can also put you in contact with others in the wider community who are less fortunate than you, allowing you to play a helping role.

EXERCISE 25

WRITE YOUR OWN PRAYER

You don't have to be religious, or even believe in a higher power, to benefit from the peace and insights that prayer can bring. This exercise will help you to tap into your spiritual side. You will need a pen and two sheets of paper.

1. Sitting quietly, close your eyes and focus inward, putting worldly thoughts aside.

2. Decide to whom you will address your prayer—for example, Lord, Father, Mother, Universe, Inner Self, and so on. Visualize them as a bright light shining down on you, enveloping you in their warmth. Feel yourself intimately connected with this force.

3. Open your eyes. Now think of something that is worrying you or any matter about which you feel you need guidance. For example, perhaps you are finding it hard to forgive someone who has hurt you, or to make an important decision. Whatever is on your mind, write down your thoughts about it.

4. Taking the second piece of paper, write your prayer. Start with your chosen addressee and then ask for help in finding within yourself the resources you need to resolve the problem—for example, compassion, empathy, and love; or clarity, insight, and inspiration. Ask with confidence and trust that your prayer will be answered.

5. Don't expect an immediate, obvious answer. Equally, don't be surprised if an unexpected solution suddenly occurs to you out of the blue. Try writing a prayer in this way whenever you need guidance.

Connecting with Others

Finding an Urban Village
EXERCISE 26: *Do a Suitability Check*

Joining a Community
EXERCISE 27: *Plug Yourself In*

Finding Others
EXERCISE 28: *Send Out Love*

Doing for Others
EXERCISE 29: *Practice Kindness*
EXERCISE 30: *Start Helping Others*

Overcoming Your Social Fears
EXERCISE 31: *Banish Social Anxiety*

Becoming More Assertive
EXERCISE 32: *Measure Your Assertiveness*

Dealing with Difficult People
EXERCISE 33: *Master Urban Judo*

Finding Romance in the City
EXERCISE 34: *Work with a Prop*

CHAPTER 4

There are times when living in a city can feel happy, even joyous. Unfortunately, there are also times when living in a city can feel lonely and isolating. The key to being truly happy in an urban environment is to build a network of social connections and develop a base of communal support.

Your relationships with others give you a sense of belonging to something larger, something more meaningful. Family, friends, and acquaintances act as stress buffers, easing the pressures of the city and providing you with support and comfort.

This chapter will show you how to become part of a welcoming neighborhood and connect with a community. It will introduce you to practical ways of meeting others, of forming meaningful relationships, and of overcoming your social fears. In short, it will help you find people you can be with, talk with, laugh with, and, at times, cry with.

Finding an Urban Village

Where you live becomes an important factor in determining just how stressful your life in the city will be. Your neighborhood should impart a sense of safety, security, and community. So, your choice of neighborhood should be a careful one. The seemingly contradictory term "urban village" best captures what you are looking for. The "urban" part suggests complexity, intensity, options, and excitement—the best of what the city has to offer. Unfortunately, it also connotes hostility, indifference, danger, and discomfort. That is why you need the "village" part. You also want simplicity, familiarity, and tranquility. You want them all.

In the past, urban villages grew in many cities, particularly where immigrants settled several generations ago. They brought with them a community spirit and a sense of belonging to a neighborhood that was welcoming and supportive. We should seek the same qualities in our cities today. The key to finding them lies in our choice of where to live. Many people don't realize what an important role their neighborhood plays in determining their day-to-day stress levels.

To find your urban village you need to look at the city differently. Rather than seeing the city as one large urban sprawl, try to see it as a patchwork of neighborhoods and communities, each with its own personality, style, and level of appeal. Unlike the suburbs or even a small town, neighborhoods in a big city can vary dramatically. In many large cities moving even a few blocks can put you in a very different environment and dramatically change in the way you experience life in the city.

Of course, your choice of neighborhood will be governed, at least to some extent, by economic factors. No matter how much you might like to live in Beverly Hills or New York's Upper East Side, such places are probably beyond your means. But there is no reason why you can't find a great neighborhood that's within your budget. Be bold. Be brazen. Ask questions and do some legwork. Check out potential areas and make a shortlist of those you like best. Next, ask people who know the city well what they think of the neighborhoods you are considering. Find out from friends and acquaintances if they know anyone who lives in those neighborhoods. If so, ask for their 'phone numbers and call them. Most of all, spend some time in the neighborhoods you are considering. Go into local stores and chat with the storekeepers. Talk to people who live in the building or block that you are thinking of moving into and look around to see who else lives there. Look for signs of friendliness.

One index of the health and vitality of a neighborhood is the number of people you see on the street, especially at weekends. Street life is the pulse of a neighborhood. You might not want to live somewhere noisy, but on the other hand city streets that are too quiet may not be what you are looking for either. You need to see your neighbors from time to time even if you may not want them as best friends. One friend who recently moved to the city found herself in a neighborhood that wasn't really a neighborhood at all. The area was dominated by commercial office buildings whose inhabitants would disappear every evening, as if by magic, when the clock struck six. Weekends found her streets pretty empty and the few services, stores, and restaurants that there were closed during that time. Yes, it was peaceful, but for my friend it was *too* quiet. She felt isolated.

When you choose your neighborhood, make sure that it has a good selection of cafés, restaurants, coffee shops, and delis—places that are people-friendly and encourage people to linger, sit, watch, and talk. The key to finding the area that is right for you is to discover enough places you find inviting—places that you know you will feel comfortable spending time in, which also attract the type of people you know you will enjoy being with.

DO A SUITABILITY CHECK

Apart from an initial "honeymoon" period when we are new to the city and we use it as our "playground," most of us spend the majority of our leisure time in our own neighborhood, so it is vital to live somewhere that meets our requirements. This exercise will help you to find the right neighborhood for you. You will need a pen and some paper.

1. Given that you will be spending most of the time when you're not working within a radius of a dozen or so blocks from your home, imagine your ideal neighborhood. What would it be like? Busy? Quiet? Trendy? What facilities would it have? Good transportation links? Good parking? Lively nightlife? A supermarket? A gas station? Taking the pen and a sheet of paper, jot down everything that you'd like to find there.

2. Now, taking another sheet of paper, draw a line down the middle to divide the page in half. Across the top write "Checklist for (name of neighborhood)." Then at the top of the left-hand column write "Essential"; at the top of the right-hand one write "Preferable." Go through items on your ideal-neighborhood list and transfer them all into one or other of the columns. The characteristics and facilities under "Essential" are your blueprint for finding the right neighborhood. Anything that comes under "Preferable" is a bonus. Take several photocopies of this checklist.

3. Each time you visit a neighborhood that you're considering, use you checklist to find out how suitable it would be. Visit all the contenders and then analyze your results. The area that has the most ticks in the "Essential" column is your frontrunner.

Joining a Community

Living in a neighborhood is not the same as living in a community. You could say that a sense of community is the intangible thread that links you to a neighborhood, or for that matter, an entire city. Communities are made up of invisible, but meaningful relationships between people. You create a community by constructing a variety of connections and involvements. These are the building blocks that ultimately turn a neighborhood into a community.

If you want to feel part of your community, the best place to start is with the local people. It can be as simple as chatting with a neighbor, nodding hello to your mailman, or joking with a local storekeeper. Make an overture. Say "Good Morning." These small, but important connections provide the basis for a feeling of connectedness that contributes to a sense of belonging.

Make sure that you patronize your local stores. This may take more time and effort, and may even cost a little more, but the payoff can easily make up for the added expense. And find out about any organizations and groups in your neighborhood that could be of interest. Ask about local churches, synagogues, or mosques; find out about residents' associations, civic groups, and any other societies or clubs where people regularly come together. Then go take a look, and if it feels right, join up.

PLUG YOURSELF IN

To become part of your urban community, you need to get involved in local activities. This exercise will help you find the right group or groups. You will need a pen and a sheet of paper.

1. Take the pen and paper. On the left-hand side of the page write a list of categories that reflect your potential interests and involvements. Be as specific as you can.

2. On the right-hand side of the page identify local classes, groups, associations, or venues in which you could pursue each interest or involvement. For example, if you enjoy playing basketball, ask around the neighborhood to find out where the local teams are based, and jot this information down.

3. Follow up each lead and try out a meeting/session/class.

My interests, hobbies, involvements	**Where/how to connect locally**
• Join a (sports) team	_____
• Share/explore a hobby	_____
• Participate in recreational activities	_____
• Join a gym	_____
• Express my religious/spiritual needs	_____
• Learn a new skill	_____
• Help the needy	_____
• Find activities for my kids	_____
• Anything else	_____

Finding Others

Connecting with others in the city might, at first thought, seem an easy matter. After all, cities are filled with people. They are all around you—from the moment you open your front door in the morning and begin your day until you return home in the evening. In fact, it might seem more difficult to escape from others than to connect with them. But even with all these people around, the reality is that it is unlikely you will know many of them who live down the block or even in your building, let alone in the wider neighborhood. All this makes meeting others, making friends, and finding partners difficult, and at times rather daunting. Yet with the right motivation and a little effort you will soon be on the right track.

Among the biggest obstacles to meeting new people in the city are our old attitudes and assumptions. These internal rules act as roadblocks, slowing us down in our quest to meet new people, and in some cases making it almost impossible to get involved with others at all. Many of these beliefs are deeply ingrained, and we are barely aware of how they operate. But they do. For example, you may be under the impression that meeting people should happen naturally and spontaneously. But in reality meeting new people in the city is often a deliberate, and sometimes contrived

SEND OUT LOVE

When we are stressed we tend to shut out other people and withdraw into our-selves. But in order to attract the right people into our lives we need to open up and send out positive signals. This exercise shows you how to send out love and good thoughts to everyone around you.

1. *Sit somewhere quiet and comfortable. Take a few slow, deep breaths to calm and relax yourself.*

2. *Think of someone close to you—for example, your partner, your child, or your best friend. Picture them in your mind. Now "send" them love and good thoughts by visualizing your feelings as a pure white light enveloping them from head to toe.*

3. *Next, conjure up an image of an acquaintance, such as the man who runs the local store or the woman you chat to at the bus stop every day. Picture them bathed in the white light of your love and good thoughts.*

4. *Now pick a complete stranger, such as a fellow subway passenger; a person in the line at the bank or the supermarket; and so on. Think of them and send them love and good thoughts in the same way. (Don't dismiss anyone simply because they were difficult or rude—if anything, such people need your love and good thoughts even more than someone who seems happy.)*

5. *As you practice sending out love and good thoughts regularly in this way, you will probably notice others reacting to you more warmly in return.*

process that can take time and effort. So, a good start is to make a conscious change in your attitude.

Make a decision to keep an open mind about meeting people. Be willing to consider going to new places and trying out new activities, no matter how outlandish, brash, or even silly they may at first seem. You don't necessarily have to embrace them all, rather just consider them. Then choose several to try out and see for yourself whether you get results.

The best way to find others is to build a lifestyle that is involving, interesting, and helps you get to know like-minded people. You come in contact with dozens of people on a daily basis, many of whom would be delighted to know you if they only had the chance. So go on, give them that chance. Fine. But you might be wondering where exactly you are supposed to find these people. Remember how we talked about ways of joining the community (see pp.90–91)? Everything described there also applies if meeting others is your goal. The difference is, you are now willing to widen your parameters and use the entire city as your hunting ground. Every city has numerous groups and organizations that can put you in contact with like-minded city-dwellers. By sharing and developing a common interest, you establish a natural bond with someone that can transform your relationship from mere acquaintances to good friends.

Apart from the groups already mentioned (see p.90) you could try your block, co-op, or condo association, or your child's school (the Parent–Teacher Asssociation or fund-raising group). Or you might prefer to join a book, nature, music, political, or singles' group—or any special-interest group that you might like to get involved in.

Another option would be to go to school. One advantage of living in the city is the access you have to the many classes and courses that are offered. You could try a new craft, take up writing or painting, learn a language or how to cook or dance. Or learn a new sport, or how to play a game; or join a sports team.

You can often find places, such as a local restaurant, a café, or a bookstore, where you can spend time and meet people. In many countries people customarily drop in at their local café and leisurely nurse a cup of coffee or tea while making conversation. It happens here too, but not enough, so revive that wonderful custom. Look for inviting cafés and coffee shops—places where you'll feel comfortable and that encourage people to linger, sit, and watch, and to strike up a conversation.

Doing for Others

The rewards for helping others are manifold. Apart from the immediate feeling of satisfaction that comes when you do something good for someone, when you give or do something for others, you often get as much—if not more—back. And, of course, if you are religious, you probably believe that you will also be rewarded in the hereafter. But there is another, less obvious reward—that benevolence can act as a stress buffer, and thus enhance your resilience to city life.

Our lives are full of uncertainty and confusion. We are all constantly searching for connections and involvements that will add value and give purpose to our existence. Helping others can offer a sense of doing something worthwhile with our own lives, and of making a genuine contribution to others' lives. When we help others we feel good about ourselves; we feel valued. Because our stress is often related to a lack of self-worth, doing for others becomes a truly valuable way of changing the way we see ourselves. If you can feel that what you are doing is contributing to the betterment of others, you then feel good about yourself being a part of that contribution.

Studies have documented some of the benefits of altruism. Researchers studied subjects who presented some of the more

PRACTICE KINDNESS

When you live in the city, it is easy to rush around without giving yourself any time to spend on the apparent non-essentials of life, such as doing something kind for a fellow human being. This exercise shows how you can incorporate a small act of kindness into a busy lifestyle. You will need a pen and some paper.

1. Take a few moments to draw up a list of individuals whom you know would benefit from a small act of kindness. Apart from including the obvious people, such as family and friends, try to think of others whom you could help. For example, an elderly neighbor, a single parent whose child goes to the same school as yours, and so on.

2. For each person on your list, think up at least one act of kindness that you could perform for them. For example, you could invite your elderly neighbor to dinner, or babysit for the single parent so that they can go out for the evening.

3. Start with one act of kindness per week, and gradually add more. Aim to perform one act of kindness every day. It needn't be anything elaborate or time-consuming— even something as simple as offering to get a colleague some lunch when you go to buy your own is an act of kindness.

4. The more acts of kindness you do, the more this behavior will become second nature to you. And the more you incorporate doing good things for others into your life, the more reciprocal acts of kindness you will benefit from.

commonly reported stress symptoms, such as headaches and back pain, and found that those individuals who spent time helping others reported a lessening of their symptoms. It would seem that their physical pain was masked by their feelings of positive involvement provided by helping others. Another study found that women who devoted time and effort to a volunteer organization lived longer than those who did not. Maybe it's better to give than receive.

Helping others almost always involves meeting people. Unless you write an anonymous check, you will certainly find that your philanthropy involves contact with other people, whether its the person or persons you are helping, or your fellow volunteers or care-givers. The act of helping adds indirectly to your social support system, and increases your sense of connectedness to the world around you. You feel less alone.

You don't have to commit yourself to regular involvement or to membership of an organization in order to be compassionate and helpful to others. Every day there are dozens of opportunities to make random acts of kindness—a small deed, a courtesy, a word of encouragement—that all work to produce positive and satisfying feelings in both you and the person or people you help.

START HELPING OTHERS

Often the biggest obstacles to doing voluntary work are figuring out what you want to do, whether you are able to do it, and how you go about doing it. This exercise will help you smooth that process.

1. Look for situations that bring you directly into contact with others who need help. Stuffing envelopes is okay, but you'll probably find greater satisfaction in a more hands-on situation. Try helping out at a local homeless shelter, at a nursing home or a daycare center for senior citizens, or at a community center for the local youth.

2. Find an involvement that can utilize a special skill or ability that you have. For example, if you are good at a particular team sport, you could coach local kids; or if you pride yourself on your command of the English language, you could teach English to new immigrants. This way you will feel that your contribution has special worth.

3. Search for a type of helping where you feel special empathy for those with whom you are working. For example, if you once benefited from support offered by a particular helpline or organization, join them and offer the same support to someone else. If you feel an emotional connection, you are more likely to keep up your good work.

4. Don't over-commit yourself. You don't have to become a Mother Teresa, or invite homeless families to live with you. Start small—you can always take on more as and when you are able. If you undertake too much from the outset, you will only add to your stress levels, not reduce them.

Overcoming Your Social Fears

For many of us, the biggest obstacle in meeting new people is overcoming our social fears. When faced with the seemingly easy task of meeting someone new, we tense, clam up, and retreat. Call it anxiety, bashfulness, or just plain shyness—it can stop us in our tracks and prevent us from meeting new people socially.

The source of most of this anxiety is our fear of rejection. Being turned down, rebuffed, or ignored is a major blow to our self-esteem and sense of self-worth. Rather than risk such an outcome, we choose to avoid the chance of being rejected. While this provides relief in the short run, in the longer run we lose out. Fortunately, there are ways of tackling our social fears.

The first step is to talk to yourself in a more reasonable, adaptive way. You already use self-talk, but what you're probably saying is how horrible it is to face rejection. Change that self-talk. Ask yourself, what's the worst that can happen? That the person will say "no" or ignore you? Tell yourself, "I can live with this."

The second step is to jump in and take a risk—even if you're feeling somewhat hesitant. When you are 97 years old, and lying on your deathbed, you won't regret taking that risk even if you *were* rejected. What you will regret, however, is not having taken more risks. So go for it!

BANISH SOCIAL ANXIETY

We often become anxious in social situations because we expect them to go badly. This exercise shows you how to cope with and change such expectations by using a visualizion to rehearse an interaction before it actually takes place.

1. Find somewhere where you will be undisturbed for at least 15 minutes. Either sit in a comfortable chair or lie down. Close your eyes and breathe slowly and deeply for about a minute to relax yourself.

2. In your mind's eye imagine a forthcoming social situation that you feel anxious about. For example, say you want to ask someone out on a date.

3. Visualize that situation—the setting, the person you want to ask out, the other people around you, the atmosphere, and most importantly, yourself and how you are feeling. Make your picture as detailed and realistic as you can.

4. Now imagine that instead of nervous or shy, you are feeling calm, relaxed, and confident. You approach the person, make small talk, and casually ask them out. They accept. How do you feel? Relieved? Happy? Euphoric, even? Bask in this positive feeling for a few moments.

5. Run through the same scenario again, but this time imagine that the person turns you down. Visualize yourself accepting this setback gracefully. It's normal to feel disappointed, but you can also feel good that you took the risk. Remember these feelings. Having "experienced" the worst outcome, you now have nothing to fear.

Becoming More Assertive

When you act in a non-assertive manner, a number of very different emotional reactions may be triggered. You might feel angry and resentful at not expressing your true feelings, or frustrated by not getting what you wanted. You might feel victimized, pushed around, and taken advantage of. You might feel less in control, and less hopeful that you are able to achieve what you would like to achieve. You might feel less positive about yourself and about how others see you. Any or all of the above negative feelings are good reasons to want to change this pattern of interaction.

Perhaps, you might think, you were born with a non-assertive personality. And you may be right. We all come into this world with an innate predisposition to be either assertive or non-assertive. But that is only the start. There are the added contributions of your parents, other influential people, such as your teachers, and your life experience. This "baggage" may seem unchangeable. The good news is that you can learn how to think differently, act differently, and, ultimately, how to feel differently.

One useful way of changing your own behavioral patterns is to observe family members, friends, and colleagues whose assertive style you admire. Try to model yourself on them. At the same time it is a good idea to monitor your own behavior. Keep a brief diary describing when you do and do not act assertively. It doesn't have to be anything elaborate—just a pocket-sized notebook that you can carry around and write about your behavior in.

Start by working on situations where you feel only minimal or moderate amounts of anxiety, and work your way up to the stuff that makes your heart pound and your hands perspire. Don't expect immediate changes. Becoming more assertive means changing a behavioral pattern that you have adopted for years. Don't be surprised if learning new ways of thinking and behaving takes a little time.

When you assert your own needs, you do not let others take advantage of you, nor do you feel guilty. You are not meek, but neither are you aggressive, and you do not blame or resent. However, being assertive is about more than being able to return a broken toaster or being able to tell a waiter that your wine is corked. Acting assertively is knowing how to express your opinions, wants, needs, and feelings in ways that do not compromise the rights of others, nor demean them in any way.

And there is another side to being assertive, one that is often overlooked—it can allow you to demonstrate your positive feelings toward someone and enable you to express affection and caring. Being assertive makes you feel comfortable when you both give and receive compliments, thank-yous, and other expressions of praise and gratitude, because it makes you feel good about yourself and your actions.

It's not just the actual words you use that convey assertiveness, it's also how you say them. The manner in which you deliver your message, and the body language that you use as you do so also need to be assertive—otherwise they may contradict the meaning of your words. The next time you are practicing assertiveness, ask yourself the following questions.

- Am I speaking in a loud, clear voice, or am I mumbling or garbling my words?
- Am I shouting or yelling?
- Is my tone sarcastic or demeaning?
- Do I sound confident or aggressive?
- Am I avoiding eye contact with the person I am talking to?
- Am I sitting or standing still while I'm speaking, or am I fidgeting around?

You can also use the above questions as a mental checklist whenever you're acting assertively, to make sure that your non-verbal behavior is congruent with your message.

MEASURE YOUR ASSERTIVENESS

The following list outlines several of the behaviors and traits that apply to unassertive people. Read each statement and rate yourself on the extent to which each statement applies to you, using the categories: "not like me," "a little like me," and "a lot like me."

- *I am very uncomfortable about expressing my needs and wants.*
- *I hate confrontations and arguments.*
- *I have trouble asking for help or a favor from others.*
- *When people ask a favor of me, I find it hard to say no.*
- *I am uncomfortable when I receive compliments and praise.*
- *In social situations, I usually let others do the talking.*
- *I find it hard to ask someone who is annoying me to stop.*
- *I have a lot of trouble speaking up in a group or in a meeting.*
- *I become anxious when I am in a conversation with people I do not know well.*
- *Those who know me have said that I am not assertive enough.*

Your score

Look at your ratings. How many fall into the "a lot like me" category? If more than one or two do, it suggests that a lack of assertiveness could be playing a significant role in creating your daily dose of urban stress.

Dealing with Difficult People

While there are many nice people who live in your city, there are many who are not so nice. Some are downright difficult. In fact, there is no shortage of difficult people to be found in any city. Take your pick from rude clerks, hostile drivers, pushy shoppers, oblivious cyclists, bad-mannered pedestrians, or difficult and unfriendly just-about-everybody. At some point you will be pushed, ignored, yelled at, kept waiting, interrupted, cut off, insulted, or otherwise treated impolitely. And while you cannot totally avoid difficult people, you can minimize your aggravation by learning how to handle them.

You can start by changing your expectations. Be more realistic. Expect to experience those things that actually do happen in life. And be ready for them to happen. Most often, we overreact when we are caught off-guard. Say, for example, someone cuts in front of you in the traffic or sneaks in ahead of you when you are waiting in a long line. Thrown off balance, you react from your gut. You feel hurt, angry, or upset. As a result, you overreact and become aggressive, or you do nothing at all and bottle up anger and resentment. If, magically, you had had advance warning that this might happen, you would have been mentally prepared and so you would have felt and reacted differently.

By anticipating a future experience or encounter, you unconsciously replace the unrealistic expectation that hostile, unfriendly, and rude behavior shouldn't and won't happen, with the more realistic acceptance that this kind of behavior does happen, will happen, and in fact happens all the time. So when something untoward does happen, you won't be caught off-guard. You will be more in control, and in a position to evaluate your options and decide sensibly the best way to respond.

When dealing with difficult people, bear in mind that you might be in the habit of "mind-reading" and "conclusion-jumping" (see p.60). Remember that we mind-read and conclusion-jump whenever we mistakenly believe that we know what someone else is thinking, or we wrongly conclude that something is so, when in fact it is not. Most of us make many, often incorrect, assumptions about other people and by so doing only create stress for ourselves. The golden rule is always to check whether you really have enough evidence to support the assumptions that you are making. If the answer is no, it is wise to reconsider and hold off coming to any premature conclusions just yet. Who knows, you may be right, but if you are like most of us, much of the time you are also wrong.

Next, stop "personalizing." You personalize when you mistakenly assume that it is your personality or behavior that triggers negative reactions in others. For example, you become upset when a fellow driver makes a nasty comment about your driving; or you become distressed when a rude sales clerk ignores you. In fact, none of this may be your fault. When you personalize, you fail to distinguish between opinion and fact. You assume that because people say something, or voice a criticism, they must be right. Of course, sometimes they will be right, but often they won't.

It is worth bearing in mind that many people who live in a city have problems. Some have personality problems, most are probably under too much stress, and the majority will have priorities that differ from yours. So before you let yourself get too distressed, stop and ask yourself, "Is this really worth getting myself upset about?"

One good way to deal with difficult people is to be totally charming, polite, and helpful in the face of their bad behavior. This often disarms them because it is the reaction they are least expecting. However, perhaps the safest option is to avoid confrontation wherever possible, and just walk away. For more on this very effective technique, see the exercise opposite.

MASTER URBAN JUDO

When I did judo as an undergraduate, the thing that impressed me most about it was the concept of *sidestepping* rather than confronting. This principle and model of engagement is also appropriate for psychological survival in a city— I call it "urban judo." Here's how to apply it.

1. Consider the following scenario. You are on your way home from work and are entering a crowded subway station. Suddenly someone pushes you from behind. You turn around, but no one apologizes, so you just think to yourself, "These things happen," and walk on. But a moment later you are pushed again, even harder, and this time you catch the guilty party. How do you feel? What do you do? Your first instinct might be to react with rage and give them a shove back. But if you follow that reaction to its logical conclusion, you could end up down at the local police precinct, or worse, in hospital. And if you think that by responding angrily or with hostility you will convince the other person to change their behavior, you are probably mistaken.

2. Run through the same scenario again in your head, but this time react the urban-judo way—when you catch the person who pushed you, take a deep breath and simply walk away. You are not being cowardly; you are not being weak; you are being sensible. You are avoiding extra stress and acting in a city-savvy way.

3. Resolve to use the urban-judo technique whenever you are faced with an unnecessary confrontation, such as when another driver cuts you off in traffic or someone barges in front of you to get on the bus.

Finding Romance in the City

It is said that everyone who lives in a city is at any one time look-ing for at least one of three things: a new place to live, a new job, or a new relationship. Of the three, most often it is the last that causes us the most stress.

I wish I could say that finding the person of your dreams is easy. Perhaps a few of us are lucky enough to meet that special him or her quite effortlessly. But for the rest of us meeting potential partners is far more arduous, far less magical, and frankly—a pain. Everything said earlier about meeting people and making new friends in the city (see pp.100–101) also applies to meeting your soulmate. The difference is, you have to be even more deter-mined, more committed, and most important more gutsy.

Explore anyplace, anywhere, anytime. Forget the notion that there is a right place and time in which to meet your ideal partner. There isn't. This means that you have to consider even the most unromantic venues as places where you might find that certain someone. Some locations that could bear fruit, even though you might think initially that they are unlikely, are: on the bus; in the supermarket check-out line; waiting for the subway; in museums; at your place of worship; at the library; in the post office; in drugstores; even in your dentist's waiting room.

Once you have spotted someone you feel you would like to meet, bite the bullet and take a risk. Make your move. Learn to flirt —flirting is the most efficient and effective way of meeting someone. By flirting I mean make eye contact (but don't stare—simply lock eyes for a brief second or two). And smile (slightly, not ear-to-ear). Then say something to the person. This goes, of course, for both men and women.

It is important to learn how to break the ice. Most of us have admired the social smoothie who, in just about any situation, is able to come up with an apt and very witty comment that immediately catapults them into the inner circle while we cower on the periphery thinking, "I wish I'd thought of that." Fortunately, you don't need to come up with a brilliant one-liner. Trying to come up with something clever might leave you frozen and mute. Or it might sound too contrived. Even worse it could be met with stony silence or embarrassed laughter. It's far safer to play safe and consider what you say as simply a way of getting your foot in the door. So don't over-think. Just ask a question or give a compliment.

Once the conversation has started you can take it anywhere else you wish. Simply start talking. Do try to make your overtures open-ended and where possible avoid questions with a yes-or-no answer. Then, assuming that there is sufficient interest, give your new acquaintance your business card and say how nice it would be if you got together for coffee or something.

Answering or putting your own ad in a "Personal" column can be an effective weapon in the war on singledom. The ad could be in a newspaper, a magazine, or even on-line. If you do arrange to meet anyone as a result of this type of contact, ensure that you meet them in a public place and that a friend or family member knows when and where you are meeting the person (who, after all, is a complete stranger). Never give out your full name, address, and 'phone number to anyone until you get to know them.

These days there are many types of dating services. As well as the traditional ones where you have an interview at an agency and are then matched up with other clients on its books, there are dating agencies that can put you in contact with potentially compatible partners through the internet. Other popular ways of meeting people for romance include "speed-dating," in which you spend an evening on a series of five-minute "mini-dates" with up to about twenty prospective partners, and lunch and dinner clubs where you get to meet like-minded individuals in the social context of an organized dinner or lunch.

WORK WITH A PROP

When we are trying to meet other men and women for the purpose of romance we need all the help we can get. Sometimes having an accessory or a prop can give a reason for someone to start a conversation with you, or you with them. Here are some field-tested suggestions, which you can try out.

1. Borrow an adorable baby or small child for the day, for example a niece or a nephew. But make it clear that they are not your child. If you don't know any suitable children, borrow a cute pet instead. Puppies are probably the most versatile because you can take them practically anywhere. Kittens and baby rabbits are also very appealing, if less portable. Stay away from reptiles.

2. If you are artistic, take a sketch pad and some pencils and install yourself in front of one of the most popular paintings in your local art gallery. Even better, if you can paint, take an easel, some paints, and a canvas and set up at a local beauty spot.

3. Borrow a camera of the type used by professional photographers and go around the city taking (or pretending to take) photographs of unusual people and objects.

4. Take your own or a borrowed laptop and use it somewhere public, such as in your local park. Be ready to answer the question, "What are you writing?"

Finding Peace and Tranquility

Your Home is Your Sanctuary
EXERCISE 35: *Achieve Harmony with Color*

Discover the Joys of Solitude
EXERCISE 36: *Create Your Personal Haven*

Diminishing the Noise
EXERCISE 37: *Sound-proof Your Home*

City Oases
EXERCISE 38: *Plant an Urban Garden*
EXERCISE 39: *Take a Quiet Moment*

The Calm Within
EXERCISE 40: *A Simple Meditation*
EXERCISE 41: *A Walking Meditation*

CHAPTER 5

A city can provide you with just about everything and anything you might want or need. Everything, that is, except a little peace and quiet, and time by yourself.

The noise in the city ranges from the simply annoying, such as the hum of ceaseless traffic, to the completely unbearable, such as the loud thumping of your next-door-neighbor's music at 3am. But there is another kind of noise that can contribute equally to urban stress—the inner whirring of your own thoughts and worries. Escaping this mental din becomes as important as escaping the other sounds of the city.

In this chapter you explore the ways in which you can minimize and avoid both noise and mental din. You learn where to find pockets of calm and tranquility and how to transform the clamor and demands of the city into a more peaceful harmony, so that you can regroup, and revitalize yourself.

Your Home is Your Sanctuary

If you live in a city, you need a sanctuary. Where you live should be a retreat, sheltering you from the chaos and confusion of the city. Your home is one of the more important factors determining just how stressful your life in the city will be. Your home should be an island of comfort—your personal space—insulating you from the chaos that lurks outside your door. Where you live need not be a palace, but it should be a refuge of sanity and serenity, a place where you can unwind and relax. When you enter your front door you should feel happy to be there. You should feel calm, content, and at peace.

There are certain homes that always feel warm and welcoming, and that put us at complete ease. Our breathing slows, our stress-levels drop, and our bodily tension diminishes as soon as we cross the threshold. Unfortunately, there is no simple formula for turning where you live into such a warm and welcoming place. However, there are common elements of structure and design that can help you achieve a greater sense of calmness and tranquility.

Color can dramatically change the way you feel about a room. By changing the color you can make a room appear larger or smaller, more formal or casual, more inviting or distant. In some rooms, for example the bedrooms, you will probably aim for peace

ACHIEVE HARMONY WITH COLOR

The colors with which we surround ourselves have a noticeable effect on our mood and feelings because they influence both our minds and our bodies. If the color of each room in your home is appropriate for its specific purpose, you create a harmonious, stress-free environment. This exercise helps you to choose the right color schemes. You will need a pen and some paper.

1. Take the pen and a sheet of paper. Make a list of the rooms in your home and describe the current color(s) of each one.

2. Now, write down what would be your ideal colorscheme for each room. Bear in mind that generally the red end of the spectrum stimulates and excites us, and the blue end calms and relaxes us. So, for your bedroom you might choose blue or green because they are restful colors; and for your living room you might select a shade of apricot or peach because they are warm hues that create the right ambience for being sociable. But there are no hard-and-fast rules when it comes to choosing a color—if you like it, go with it. Always choose colors that work for you, not ones that you think others will approve of—after all, you have to live with them. Keep the details of your chosen color scheme somewhere safe until you are ready to decorate.

3. Begin with the room that most needs a makeover. Buy a sample pot of paint to test out the new color first on a small section of wall. And check what it looks like at different times, in both daylight and with artificial lighting. Once you are sure that you are happy with it, buy the paint and get started.

and relaxation. In others, such as the dining room, you may prefer intensity and excitement. Try to find a balance in your color scheme. Lighter colors can create a feeling of openness and greater space. More intense colors can work well in smaller rooms. For more on color, see the exercise on page 117.

The way in which you light your home is an important factor that can enhance the warmth and emotional feeling of your space. Imaginative lighting can create a sense of intimacy and drastically improve the feeling of a room. One way of inducing warmth is to position lamps of lower wattage at different places around a room. This gives the place an overall glow, especially if you add lampshades in warm hues. You can also use decorative lighting to highlight a painting, a bookshelf, or a corner of a room adding to the interest and visual texture. And simply by installing a dimmer switch you have the facility to change the mood of a room instantly and dramatically.

Mirrors are a useful tool in opening up your space. Carefully positioned—say, in a narrow hallway, or above a mantel—they give an impression of room and airiness. You can use mirrors not only to make smaller spaces appear larger, but also to bring additional sunlight into a normally drab room.

Sometimes it is the little, personal touches that add feelings of warmth and connectedness to our homes. Apart from the obvious things, such as photographs of family members and friends, a cherished collection of books can be both comforting and inspiring. Around your house you can probably find items that remind you of good times and pleasures past—souvenirs of happy vacations; paintings or *objets d'art*, such as vases, pottery, or miniatures; and so on. And don't underestimate the power of houseplants and fresh flowers to bring a ray of sunshine into a home. Their presence can create a feeling of serenity and can instantly turn your living space into a place of beauty.

Candles, besides providing some light, can add an air of romance, tranquility and coziness to your home with their soft glow. The flickering of the flame can be hypnotic and relaxing. Particularly popular these days are scented candles, which can calm or invigorate you depending on the essential oils they contain. Some of the more common scents you can use to promote a relaxed, calm state include lavender, rose, chamomile, vanilla, bergamot, geranium, and sandalwood. For a more energizing effect you can try citrus (grapefruit, orange, and lime), jasmine, pine, and patchouli.

Discover the Joys of Solitude

If you live in a city, one of the hardest things to find is a place where you can be all by yourself. Not everyone, of course, seeks or wants solitude. In fact, these days the concept of solitude has developed a negative, anti-social connotation. Yet being alone, as many of us know, can be glorious. Being in your own head—daydreaming, planning, imagining—away from everyone, can be incredibly involving and wonderfully satisfying. Being by yourself allows you to recenter. It lets you put the stresses of the world in perspective and assess what is truly important in your life. True, city solitude may last only for a few minutes, but those minutes can go a long way.

Learning to appreciate solitude and time for yourself takes practice. Start gradually. Reading by yourself is often a good way to begin, but choose a book that you know you will like. Find a place that is quiet and relatively free of other people. Settle in and get comfortable. Make sure you turn off the TV, radio, and anything that might be distracting, such as your 'phone. Now read quietly, savoring the peacefulness. Once you are comfortable with this, try being alone without the book. Listen to music or just sit and think—it's incredibly relaxing. Appreciating solitude can be an acquired pleasure, but it is one well worth the effort.

CREATE YOUR PERSONAL HAVEN

Although space is at a premium in city dwellings, it is important that you have your own haven—somewhere in your home where you can relax and be by yourself. This will be your inner sanctum, a place to which you can retreat when you want to read, write, think, or just daydream.

1. Choose the place where you will make your haven. If you don't have the luxury of a spare room, don't worry. Your haven could be somewhere as simple as a window-nook, or perhaps a corner in a warm kitchen, an inviting bedroom, or a cozy study where you can close the door and feel away from it all.

2. Make your haven as inviting as possible. Have somewhere comfortable to sit; decorate your area with a special photograph or picture, a vase of fresh flowers, or a favorite object. You could also keep a scented candle or incense to burn when you retreat there and a portable CD player to play relaxing music on. If you intend to do any writing in your haven, keep a notebook or journal to hand.

3. Designate this space as your retreat—a place where you don't worry, don't pay bills, don't answer the 'phone, or do anything else that could even remotely increase your stress levels.

4. Spend time in your haven at least once a day. If you feel that you are generally much too busy to find time to do this, there is even more reason why you should pencil in some time for yourself in your sanctuary to relax by doing whatever you wish.

Diminishing the Noise

If you plan on living in a city, you'd better make noise a major consideration. A quiet city is a contradiction of terms. Cities are, by their very nature, noisy places. The only time I can remember my city being totally quiet is right after a major snowfall. Then, there is little or nothing happening on the streets. Sounds normally heard—the few trucks, cars, or people who venture out—are gently muffled by a blanket of snowy insulation. The effect is surreal and timeless. Most other times the city is rarely quiet. There is a constant din created by car horns, car alarms, police sirens, firetruck sirens, screeching brakes, garbage trucks, never-ending construction and road repair. And that's just outside.

Indoors it can be worse. Boisterous party-loving neighbors, successful musicians and singers, unsuccessful musicians and singers, or simply someone next door who is heavy-handed with the hi-fi or TV volume control can make your life a living hell.

Too often when we buy or rent we give too little attention to just how noisy our new place will be. While you should expect to have to live with noise in a city, you don't want to discover that noise is making your life even more stressful than it already is. You want to be able to sleep at night, and hear the sound of your own 'phone ringing.

When you are checking out an apartment or a house that you are considering as a future home, try to find out just how noisy living there will be. The key is to ask, look, and, most important, listen. Start by asking the present occupants and any friendly people who live in the neighborhood about their experiences with noise. Look out for nearby businesses with noisy ventilating systems or air conditioners. Also see if there are any clubs, cafés, and restaurants in the vicinity—they may be silent all day, but become unbelievably noisy at night, so try to visit your prospective home at different times of the day. When you are there, listen for unusually noisy neighbors and find out if any babies or young children live nearby—they can be heard as well as seen. And notice the level of noise from passing traffic, which, of course, might also vary according to the time of day or night.

But what can you do once you've already moved in and you are faced with disruptive noise? One effective way of dealing with low-key but persistent noise is to mask it. The secret of masking is to find a more tolerable noise and use it to "cover" the one that you don't wish to hear. For example, you could mask the sound of your neighbor sanding their floors by playing music. You can also get tapes or CDs featuring just about any sound you might find relaxing—waves crashing onto the shore, rain-forest sounds, or a gurgling brook. Find one that can provide a soothing background and mask any unwanted sounds.

For louder, more intermittent noise, stronger tactics are sometimes called for. A heavy metal music fan who lives upstairs and blasts out their music or a deafening sanitation truck outside your window at the crack of dawn may call for a more radical approach, such as the wearing of earplugs. However, you don't want to have to wear earplugs for the rest of your days. Sometimes complaining is the best solution. Most neighbors are reasonable people who will make every effort to diminish the amount of noise that they make, once you point out that it is excessive or upsetting. Often people don't realize just how much sound can travel.

Of course, having neighbors who seem heedless of your requests for quiet, or finding (all to late) that you are living close to a noisy bar may require other action. Fortunately, there are laws that regulate noise levels. Every large city has a Department of Environmental Protection, or its equivalent, that investigates serious complaints and can issue legally-enforceable noise abatement orders. However, thankfully, having to resort to such extreme measures is a rarity.

SOUND-PROOF YOUR HOME

If you are finding it hard to live with the the level of noise you are subjected to in your home, try this exercise. You will need a pen and some paper.

1. Look around your home, room by room, and try to determine exactly where most of the disruptive noise comes from. Write down what you believe to be the prime source of noise in each room.

2. Analyze the results. For example, windows overlooking a busy street are often the prime culprit for letting in noise from the outside, because even if you keep them shut a lot of sounds still seem to be able to get through.

3. Think of ways to reduce the noise. For example, if your windows are the problem, the best solution is probably to install double-pane glass. If this is too expensive or impractical and is not an option, consider getting heavy drapes or shutters instead— these will deaden the noise and perhaps even make the room look better. Bear in mind that similarly carpets, rugs, wall hangings, pictures, bookcases, and bookshelves can all be introduced into various rooms to help absorb excess noise.

4. Don't be afraid to find creative solutions. For example, if your bedroom is particularly noisy but your living room is quieter, swap them around. This might involve some time and ingenuity, and a certain amount of disruption, but the undisturbed sleep you will gain as a result will be well worth the effort.

City Oases

Privacy and seclusion are hard to come by once you leave your home. True solitude, in the sense of complete isolation, is very hard to find in an urban environment. However, relative solitude and a greater sense of seclusion, privacy, and quiet are possible to find—even if there are a few other people around.

A park is a natural space in which to seek solitude and calm. Every major city has many wonderful parks where you can stroll aimlessly or become lost in your own thoughts. Walking through the park on your way to the office or coming home after work is a wonderful way of mellowing out and disengaging from the city. Make an effort to get to know many of the nicer parks in your city. Mini-parks are far more numerous. Sometimes they are no more than a small patch of grass, a few trees, and a bench or two. But on the right day and at the right time, they can be relatively empty and provide you with some peace and quiet.

We tend to think of houses of worship as religious sanctuaries and as places for prayer. They are, of course, but churches and temples can also be visited for non-religious expression. You can reflect, meditate, or simply lose yourself in reverie. They are quiet and softly lit—ideal settings in which to be alone. Many are quite majestic and sweeping in their architectural grandeur,

PLANT AN URBAN GARDEN

The word paradise comes from the Persian-cum-Greek *paradeisos*, meaning "the private park of kings"—a place where there was peace and tranquility amid the fruit trees and beautiful flowers.

1. In the city where space is at a premium, it can seem impossible to find room for a garden. But, even a small space on a patio, a window ledge, or a rooftop can give you enough space in which to grow some flowers or plants. And if there is nowhere outside, you could grow a small herb garden in the kitchen or keep several houseplants.

2. If you are planting a garden outside, make sure that you choose flowers and shrubs that flourish in your climate. For example, if you live in a dry, semi-arid climate, grow plants that need very little water, such as cacti. Or, if you live somewhere temperate, choose hardy plants—survivors that can hold their own against periods of inclement weather.

3. If you lead a very busy life and don't have much leisure time, make a small indoor garden featuring low-maintenance plants, such as Aspidistras, rubber plants, and spider plants. Or cultivate decorative miniature trees, such as dwarf pines or Japanese bonsai trees.

4. For in-depth advice on what to grow, consult your local plant store. They will know exactly what would work well either in- or outside your house or apartment.

inspiring and revitalizing even the most city-worn spirit. And don't forget city cemeteries, which tend to be overlooked as natural venues for seclusion. They are almost always uncommonly quiet and can be surprisingly uplifting. There you can do some of your best thinking and daydreaming.

Many cities are located on the shores of oceans, lakes, or rivers. One of the reasons they got started as cities was that they were accessible by water. With a bit of scouting you can usually discover a quiet area overlooking the water. Watching the sun rise or set over water can be wonderfully tranquilizing.

Zoos and aquariums make excellent places in which to escape most humans, especially if you go on a week-day. Unlike some of the people you know, most animals will make you laugh or smile; and watching beautifully colored fish swim slowly and elegantly can be very relaxing.

Other great places for peace and quiet include public libraries—their large tables, vast spaces, and enforced silence make them ideal places to work, think, and imagine. Similarly, some bookstores, with their spacious floors lined with wonderful books, become an inviting setting to which you can often retreat at off-peak times. Consider them your private libraries.

TAKE A QUIET MOMENT

You may think that in order to relax you need plenty of time. Ideally, this is so, but sometimes even a few snatched moments of escape can bring us respite. These mini-retreats can act as important stress buffers, refreshing our souls and re-energizing our bodies. This exercise shows you how you can steal a brief moment or two for reflection or relaxation in the most unexpected places.

1. Most of us carry a photo of a loved one or of close family members in our wallet or purse. When you are waiting for the bus or subway to and from work, or sitting in the doctor's or dentist's waiting room, get out your photo and study it. Think of the person or people in it. Recall the happy time when the photo was taken, or a fun occasion you recently enjoyed together. This is guaranteed to put a smile on your face and make you feel more relaxed.

2. When you are driving, tension often builds up in your neck and shoulders. While you are waiting for traffic to clear or even for the signals to change, grab a moment to lift your shoulders up toward your ears several times and then slowly lower them again. This will help release tension in the shoulder and neck region.

3. While you are waiting for the elevator, or standing in line at the bank or supermarket, close your eyes for a moment and slow your breathing. As you breathe in feel your abdomen expand and your lungs fill with air. As you breathe out, imagine that, along with the air, you are ridding yourself of all tension. Continue breathing in this way for 2 minutes or longer, if possible.

The Calm Within

Peacefulness is our innate mode of being. It is how nature intended us to be because we all have the ability to create inner calm and tranquility. Mistakenly, we may believe that in order to *be* peaceful it is necessary to find a place outside ourselves that *is* peaceful. As we have seen, finding that tranquil oasis in the city, while possible, is not the easiest of tasks (see pp.126–8). The good news is, you do not have to; you can learn how to tap into your inner well of quietude at any time.

Since ancient times many in the East—especially those who adhere to traditional religious or philosophical beliefs—have been aware of our ability to find peace within. For thousands of years they have looked inward for solitude and have been able to tune out the demands of the world around them. Such contemplation and meditative practices have not been as widely embraced in the West. It seems that doing nothing makes us nervous. We value being busy and we value accomplishment. Lengthy periods of immobility tend to elicit feelings of boredom and restlessness. Unfortunately, all too often we lack the inclination or the tools to find our inner calm.

There are many paths to inner peace. However, of all of the ways that are available to us, meditation is probably the one that

A SIMPLE MEDITATION

The most common complaint among novice meditators is that their minds keep wandering. If this happens to you, don't worry—it's perfectly normal. Start meditating for just 5 minutes at a time and gradually build up to 20 minutes, as you keep practicing.

1. Find a quiet place where you won't be disturbed for a while. No telephones, no beeper, no television, no distractions of any kind. Make sure that you are sitting comfortably because you are going to remain in one position for at least 5 minutes.

2. Focus inwardly. Concentrate on a sound, a word, a sensation, an image, an object, or a relaxing thought. Soothing words such as "peace," "love," "calm," or simply the word "one" can work well. Choose a word or sound that has a calming feel. A pleasing image or object can be equally effective.

3. Maintain your focus and adopt a passive, accepting attitude. Intrusive thoughts or images will probably enter your consciousness and distract you from your focus. When such distractions appear, notice of them, and then let them pass away. Let these thoughts or images go. If they reappear, try not to get upset or annoyed. Simply refocus on your calming sound, image, or object, and let a feeling of peace and tranquility envelop you totally.

evokes the most interest—and suspicion. In the past, many Westerners have dismissed meditation as foreign and remote, and hence not for them.

However, recently researchers have started taking notice of the positive effects of meditation and its principles and practice are now generating enthusiasm and gaining acceptance in the West. In fact, it is likely that most of us have already meditated without even knowing. At those times when your mind becomes calm, uncluttered, and focused, when you are not reflecting on your day, nor thinking about a million and one things, you are doing something that closely resembles meditating.

The benefits of meditating are wide and varied. Meditative and other contemplative approaches allow you to develop greater control over your thoughts, worries, and anxieties. Most importantly, meditation can relax both your mind and your body. It can help you still your thoughts and release tension from your body, so that you are less stressed. When you practice you will notice many benefits immediately, while others will take longer to become apparent. As your practice develops you should feel rested, renewed, and recharged. Meditation is a skill, that, once mastered, will serve you well throughout your life.

A WALKING MEDITATION

When many Westerners think of meditation they conjure up an image of someone sitting cross-legged on the floor in the lotus position. However, not all meditation is static. In this exercise you learn the Zen practice of *kinhin* or walking meditation.

1. Find a quiet place where you can walk forward in a straight line for about 10 feet (3 m) without turning.

2. Keeping your thumb inside, make a fist with your left hand and place it against your body just above the navel. Cover your fist tightly with your right hand.

3. Now take a small, very slow step, as if you are walking in slow motion. Bring your right foot forward, and place it down heel first, to align with the toes of your left foot. Focus on the slow movement of your leg, and the transfer of weight from one foot to the other. Repeat the step in the same way with your left foot.

4. Keep walking until you reach the end of the prescribed distance of 10 feet (3 m), and then turn around and retrace your steps.

5. Continue walking up and down in this way for at least 5 minutes. Don't worry if at first you feel rather wobbly or impatient. With practice, you will realize that *kinhin* can help you learn to release bodily tension and to focus your mind as you move around.

Staying Healthy

If cities came with a warning label, this might read: "Living here could damage your health." An urban lifestyle makes it difficult to eat the right things, to sleep for an adequate number of hours, and to exercise as much as we should. But the irony is that we need to be in excellent health in order to cope with the stresses and strains of urban life, or we become susceptible to illness. So by neglecting yourself you could be putting your health and well-being seriously at risk. However, that's only half the story. When you don't take proper care of yourself, your own body can become a source of stress. If you are tired or run-down you become a poor stress manager.

In this chapter you discover how to become more physically resilient to the demands and pressures of the city through good nutrition, exercise, and improving your sleep. You also learn how to become healthier and how to stay that way.

Eat Well, Be Well

If you're like most city people, your eating habits are probably hit and miss—inconsistent, rushed, and made to fit around a busy schedule. For most of us, our eating style probably falls somewhere between grabbing a hot dog on a street corner and sitting down to a business lunch at a fancy restaurant. However, many of us would not earn a gold star from a nutritionist for what and how we eat. And eating the wrong things, or eating at the wrong times, can add to our stress levels.

So what can you do to help make your eating more stress-effective? Start by eating smaller meals. When you have a big meal, your body needs to divert extra blood from the vital organs, such as the brain, to help digest the food. But in so doing, the body deprives the brain of some of the oxygen it needs to keep you alert, making you feel lethargic. The solution? Graze like a cow. Spread out your eating evenly throughout the day and avoid huge meals that leave you feeling ready for a nap. Instead, eat smaller, lighter meals at regular times and supplement them with healthy snacks. Have a good breakfast, followed by a mid-morning snack. Then, have a light lunch, another snack—such as fruit—later in the afternoon, and a moderate dinner. A final light snack later in the evening should avert any hunger pangs before bedtime.

ANALYZE YOUR EATING HABITS

If you want to try to eat more healthily, it is a good idea first to analyze your current eating habits, so that you can see where you are going wrong. In this exercise, you keep a detailed food journal for 2 weeks to help you identify where there is room for improvement. You will need a pen and a small notebook.

1. Write today's date at the top of the first page. Each day for the next 2 weeks, you are going to write down everything you eat and the time at which you eat it. That includes snacks and drinks, as well as meals. If possible, write down each item just after you eat it, but if this is impractical, update your record at every mealtime. Be honest—the idea is to build up a true picture of what you eat and when you eat it.

2. Once you have collected your 2 weeks' worth of data, start your analysis. Begin by reading through everything—you might be surprised at just how much you do eat without realizing. Then, look out for any patterns that emerge. For example, perhaps you skip breakfast too often, or you tend to snack on cookies in the afternoon.

3. Highlight any areas that you feel you could improve. For example, if you are not eating the recommended 5 portions of fruit and vegetables per day, make a conscious effort to do so. Or if you feel that you are drinking too much wine, try to limit your intake to a glass or two with dinner at the weekends.

4. Make sure that you have fresh fruit and healthy snacks available at work. And plan ahead. If, say, you know you are going to the movies, take your own snacks with you, so you don't need to buy candy or a soda when you get there.

Try to include some complex carbohydrates, such as pasta, cereals, potatoes, or brown rice in every meal, as these foods can enhance your performance when you are under stress. Foods rich in carbohydrates also increase your levels of serotonin, which gives us that feel-good factor. Reduce your intake of simple carbohydrates, such as cake, cookies, soda, and candy, which can give you a short-term boost, but send your blood-sugar levels yo-yoing up and down in the long run.

Make sure that you eat adequate amounts of protein. This means eating more fish, chicken, other lean meats, or pulses and nuts. Foods high in protein enhance mental function and supply essential amino-acids that help repair your body's cells. Beans, bell peppers, carrots, squash, and green leafy vegetables are rich sources of stress-busting vitamins and nutrients. And have plenty of potassium, which is found in milk, bananas, whole grains, wheat germ, and nuts, as this mineral helps your muscles relax.

Most of us don't drink enough water. Nutritionists recommend that we drink eight glasses a day to keep ourselves hydrated and functioning optimally—that's in addition to coffee and tea, which are diuretics. If this sounds daunting, start with two or three glasses of water and gradually build up to eight.

MASTER THE ART OF EATING OUT

We urbanites love to eat out. And one of the advantages of living in a city is the vast number and wide range of restaurants we have to choose from. However, when you are trying to eat what is good for you, eating out can be a nutritional minefield. This exercise shows you how to select the healthier options.

1. Think about what you would like to eat before you get inside the restaurant. If your chosen place displays their menu outside, take a moment to make a mental shortlist of your favorites before you go in.

2. Always try to pick food that is good for you, as well as tasty. This doesn't mean confining yourself to salads. For example, choose chicken or turkey and tuna or oily fish, such as salmon, over red meat, and a selection of seasonal vegetables; or have pasta, but avoid sauces that are heavy in saturated fats, such as butter and cream. Choose whole grain bread and pasta, and brown rice wherever possible, as they contain more nutrients. And, if you absolutely must have, say, a portion of French fries, eat only half or split a regular order with your companion or someone else in your party.

3. Watch out for "menu weakness." This moment of dining insanity strikes when you have ordered a perfectly healthy dish—and then, impulsively, you cast caution to the wind by, say, smothering your food in high-cholesterol mayonnaise; or by following it with a calorie-laden dessert.

4. Stick to the above guidelines as a general rule, but do allow yourself to have free rein from time to time, particularly on special occasions and at family gatherings.

Coping with Emotional Eating

Do you often feel a need to eat when you are not physically hungry? Do you eat when you get anxious, upset, worried, or dep-ressed? If so, perhaps you are an "emotional eater." Although emotional eaters still can be prone to overeating when they are happy, it's when they feel distressed that they are likely to do the most damage.

Emotional eating can become a destructive cycle. When we feel stressed we don't necessarily choose the most healthy foods. Negative emotions distort our ability to think sensibly and we look for "comfort" foods. And, unfortunately, comfort foods tend to be those that are not good for the body, such as chocolate, ice cream, cake, donuts, and cookies. While such foods might make you feel better in the short term, once you have eaten them you often feel worse. Then, your stress returns—with additional guilt for overindulging—and you feel the need for another bout of eating. The cycle then repeats itself.

The first step in breaking the cycle is to become aware of exactly when you are distressed, and identify and label your feelings. When you feel the urge to open the refrigerator door, or before you put any food in your mouth, stop, and take stock of your emotional state. Ask yourself, "Am I really hungry or am I feeling distressed?" If you are truly hungry, eat. Otherwise acknowledge your feelings, by admitting that you are upset, nervous, or anxious, and so on. Simply breaking the stress–eating connection for even a moment can give you a different perspective and increased motivation to investigate the underlying cause of your emotional eating.

One of the best things you can do to take your mind off food is to involve yourself in an activity you enjoy. A good ploy is to leave the house. You could go for a walk, or run an errand, or visit a friend. By simply changing your environment you can rid yourself of old eating triggers. If you don't want to go out, you could read a good book; or watch an interesting TV program; or even cook. The latter suggestion may seem like asking for trouble, but often the process of cooking takes away our appetite for the food once it is ready. Even if this does not apply to you, if you make something like a soup or a casserole—a dish that is filling, and takes time to cook—you will have a fair wait before you can eat it. And who knows, by then your mood may well have changed, and instead of eating it you can freeze it for future consumption.

Another effective idea to distract yourself from food is to get some exercise. Strange as it may first seem, exercising can reduce your appetite. Hit the stationary bike or treadmill, or simply do some floor exercises, such as sit-ups or some stretching (for more on exercise, see pp.144–7).

Whenever you are about to open the refrigerator to calm frayed nerves, consider substituting a relaxation break. Try some simple deep breathing, or some muscle relaxation (see pp.22–3), or perhaps a visualization (see pp.28–31). Or play yourself some relaxing music—popular classical music, such as Beethoven's *Pastoral Symphony*, Chopin's *Nocturnes* or Handel's *Water Music* is often effective. Of course, other types of music, such as ambient can be equally soothing. Keep experimenting to find what works best for you.

You could also try working with a stress-cue. Stick a picture of yourself on your refrigerator door or on the cupboard in which you keep your goodies, as a reminder to question whether you are really hungry before you open them. Sometimes a little prompt goes a long way. You could take this one step further: Reward yourself with a small (non-food) treat every time you resist emotional eating, and "fine" yourself every time you succumb to it—put aside a coin to give to charity, or make yourself do a household chore that you've been putting off.

SNACK TO FIGHT STRESS

Many of us react to stress by reaching for food—and it's usually something unhealthy. But a candy bar or a bag of chips won't alleviate stress. The key is to include in your diet plenty of foods that not only don't *add* to your stress levels, but that also help *reduce* them. This exercise offers some useful guidelines.

1. Avoid high-sugar treats—they may taste good, but they consist largely of empty calories and they play havoc with your blood-sugar levels.

2. Stick with snacks that contain some energy-boosting proteins and are high in complex carbohydrates. They'll give you longer-lasting, sustained energy.

3. Choose quick bites and snacks from the suggestions below—these can help alleviate and counteract your stress.

- *a glass of fresh orange or grapefruit juice*
- *a piece of fruit*
- *a bowl of whole grain cereal with a sliced banana*
- *a cup of herbal tea, such as chamomile*

- *a soft pretzel*
- *an avocado and spinach salad*
- *a turkey sandwich on whole wheat bread*
- *a tuna and salad sandwich on whole wheat bread*

- *a small bowl of pumpkin soup*
- *a pot of low-fat yogurt*
- *a handful of mixed nuts*
- *a small bowl of popcorn*
- *an English muffin (but go easy on the butter or margarine)*

A Matter of Exercise

Exercise is one of the best ways of helping us cope with stress. Sustained activity—in whatever form—can decrease your blood pressure, lower your heart rate, and slow your breathing—all actions that reduce stress. Exercise is a natural and effective way of slowing, and even reversing, the body's "fight-or-flight" response. When you exercise vigorously your body produces endorphins that lift your mood and relax you.

If the word "exercise" puts you off, try substituting the word "activity." This word exchange is more than semantics. Any increase in physical activity—whether aerobic, such as jogging, or non-aerobic, such as stretching—contributes positively to your state of physical well-being. You don't need to go to a gym or a health club. You could do something as simple as walking.

As a form of exercise, walking has always had low status. That's too bad because if you do it consistently, and for a sustained period of time, it can be a terrific way of staying in shape. Walking is also a great way to clear your head and calm your mind. Why not park your car a little farther from your train station or office than usual, and walk the rest of the way? The good thing about walking is that it can be disguised as strolling or sight-seeing, which are both pleasant activities. And if you

STRETCH AND REACH FOR THE SKY

Stretching is a great way to release any tension that has accumulated in your muscles. In this exercise I have created a mini work-out incorporating some of my favorite stretches.

1. The Cherry-picker *Sit in a chair, with your feet flat on the floor. Raise both your arms up over your head and point your fingers toward the ceiling. Now pretend to reach and pick a cherry on a branch that just slightly exceeds your reach. Stretch that hand an inch (2.5cm) or so, and then make a fist. Squeeze for 2 or 3 seconds. Relax your hand. Do the same with your left hand. This stretch works your shoulders, your arms, and your back.*

2. The Pec Stretch and Squeeze *Either sit or stand up straight. Put your hands behind your head with your fingers interlaced. Try to bring your elbows back as far as you can. Hold the tension for 5 to 10 seconds, then release it. This stretch is good for relieving tightness in your shoulders, your pectoral muscles, and your upper back.*

3. The Leg Lift *Sitting in a chair, put your legs together and out in front of you, with your heels resting on the floor. Curl your toes toward you and lift your legs as high as you can, still keeping them straight out in front of you. Hold the tension for 5 to 10 seconds, and then let your feet fall to the floor. This stretch relieves tension in your quadriceps (in the thighs) and strengthens your abdominal muscles.*

venture a little further and crank up the pace a bit, you will find yourself "power-walking"—a wonderfully simple yet effective form of aerobic exercise.

Stair-climbing may not be an Olympic event, but it is a great form of exercise. Research has shown that by climbing stairs for a mere six minutes a day, you can extend your life by up to two years. The better news is, if you life in a big city, you encounter lots of stairs every day. So give the elevator or the escalator a miss and take the stairs at every opportunity.

The key to exercising successfully is to choose a type of activity that you enjoy. If you try to make yourself do something you dislike, you are probably not going to stay with it. It could be a sport, such as tennis, bowling, baseball, basketball, football, and so on. Or it could be a favorite activity, such as horseback-riding, dancing, trampolining, swimming, or ice-skating, or anything else that gets your body moving. Even gardening, if kept up for a while without stopping, can be considered a form of exercise. Cycling or roller-blading are terrific forms of exercise. Find a place where you can cycle or roller-blade safely and enjoyably, such as a large park. And always make sure that you wear the appropriate safety gear for your chosen activity.

DANCE YOUR CARES AWAY

Dancing is one of the most joyful and natural forms of human physical expression, and what's more, it's a great way to release tension. This exercise shows you how to dance away your stress. (You can do it alone if you prefer, or invite a friend or family member to join in.)

1. Look through your music collection and pick out some of your favorite, upbeat CDs. Try to include a cross-section of your musical tastes so that you always have something to hand that reflects your mood, whether they range from rock to reggae, or country to classical. Put your dance CDs to one side, where you can find them easily.

2. Choose one CD and play it. Standing in the middle of the room, close your eyes for a moment while you listen to the rhythms. Then, open your eyes and let your body gently respond to the music in whatever way comes naturally. Sway, bounce, wiggle— let yourself go! It doesn't matter what you do, or how you look. The idea is to express yourself spontaneously and unselfconsciously. Dance in this way for about 5 minutes.

3. Now, starting with your head and neck, move, shake, and loosen each part of your body in turn, in time with the music. Work down through your shoulders to your arms, hands, and fingers, and then your back and hips. Continue with your legs, feet, and toes. Finish off by shaking and loosening your whole body at once.

4. Resume dancing as you did in step 2 for at least another 5 minutes, longer if you like. Notice how your movements are more fluid now and you feel more relaxed.

5. Whenever you feel stressed, just put on a CD and dance your cares away.

Getting a Good Night's Sleep

Sleep is often the first casualty of stressful urban living. If you live in a city, chances are that you frequently feel more tired than you would like. Sometimes it's our stressful jobs that wear us out, but often it's simply that we don't manage to get enough quality sleep. Unfortunately, when you are tired your emotional threshold is lowered, and you are more vulnerable to stress. And as stress tends to breed more stress, it becomes very important to break the cycle and start getting that much-needed sleep.

Just how much sleep should you get? Most Americans are now getting between sixty and ninety minutes less per night than they need for optimal health and performance. Although most people need about seven or eight hours sleep a night, twenty per cent of all Americans get less than six hours sleep, and fifty per cent get less than eight hours. The general rule of thumb is, if you need an alarm clock to get up in the morning, you are probably not getting enough sleep. A better indicator would be simply noticing how tired you feel both during and at the end of the day.

The best sleep comes from having a regular sleep pattern. Your body's internal clock becomes stabilized with routine. This means getting to bed at the same time and getting up at the same time. Unfortunately, if you live in a city, this is easier said than

FENG-SHUI YOUR BEDROOM

Feng Shui is the ancient Chinese art of enhancing and harmonizing our surroundings by balancing the universal forces of *yin* (passive) and *yang* (active) energy in our homes. In this exercise you learn how to apply the principles of Feng Shui to your bedroom to help improve your sleep.

1. According to Feng Shui the ideal bedroom should be regular in shape—for example, square or rectangular—so the first step is to check the shape of your own bedroom. If it is neither square nor rectangular, you can "correct" its shape by putting a mirror in a place where it will reflect a corner into the space where one should be.

2. For energy to flow around a room it must be free from clutter. Take a good look at your bedroom. Are there any objects, such as a computer or an ironing board, that have no place in a sleeping environment? If so, move them elsewhere. The Feng Shui ideal is to have little else in your bedroom other than your bed, so try to keep the amount of possessions here to a minimum. Put your clothes and toiletries away in cupboards—that way, they are out of sight but still accessible.

3. Your bed should be raised off the floor on legs, to enable energy to flow all around you while you sleep. In Feng Shui it is said that energy flows directly between windows and doors, and between two doors, so it is best to avoid positioning your bed in these areas. Try to place your bed so that as you lie in it you can see anyone enter the room.

4. For optimal sleep, always keep the area where your head lies uncluttered. Never place a mirror opposite the bed as this reflects energy back at you while you sleep.

done. Getting up at the same time may be possible, but hitting the mattress at the same time every night is not that easy in the city. However, try to stick to a regular bedtime as often as possible.

Ideally, you want to establish a set of cues and habits that promote an effective sleep routine. The relationship in your mind should be bedroom = sleep. At a certain hour designate the bedroom a place where you wind down and relax. This means banning upsetting discussions, work, household paperwork, arguments, unpleasant 'phone-calls, or anything else that might trigger worry, anxiety, and stress. You can read, write your journal (if you have one), meditate, or do whatever else you usually do to relax your body and still your mind.

The quality of your sleep is as important as the number of hours you sleep, and caffeine and alcohol can both have an adverse effect. Most people know that coffee contains caffeine and they should avoid drinking it before bedtime, but how many of us are also aware that there is caffeine in many teas, colas, and even chocolate, so they too should be avoided? With alcohol, drinking a little, such as a nightcap, can actually help you sleep, but greater amounts will only disrupt your sleep patterns and leave you feeling tired and dehydrated when you wake up.

STOP ANXIOUS THOUGHTS

There are times when we can't fall asleep at night because the worries and concerns of daily life keep our minds racing and our bodies restless. This exercise will show you a technique that can help you in such situations.

1. When you are trying to get to sleep and you catch yourself dwelling on problems or nagging concerns, tell yourself firmly, "I don't want to worry about this right now!"

2. Close your eyes and mentally conjure up a red-and-white road sign—the kind that says "STOP." Blow up the sign In your mind so that it is large and vivid. Now silently, in your own head, shout the word "STOP!" The image of the sign and the verbal "STOP" command will disrupt your thought-sequence and temporarily put the worry out of your mind.

3. Find a relaxing thought or image that you can substitute for the one you've been worrying about. Your thought or image can be anything that you find relaxing. For example, you could picture yourself lying in a hammock in an imaginary tropical paradise or recall an anecdote that makes you smile. The idea is take your mind completely away from your problems and help your body to relax.

4. Don't be disheartened if the worrisome thoughts reappear. This is annoying but perfectly normal. Just repeat steps 1 to 4 until your mind calms and your body feels more settled. And before you know it you will fall sound asleep.

Thriving in the City

Staying Safe

Getting Close to Nature

Rediscovering Your City

Savoring the Smaller Pleasures

Discovering Urban Getaways

Although most of us would agree that a city has the ability to enchant, charm, and amuse us, we would also agree that once the honeymoon ends, the realities of day-to-day existence can rob us of that delight and enjoyment.

In this chapter, you learn how to find the right balance between coping with urban demands and strains, and deriving pleasure from the very things that make a city a city. You discover how to get to know the city. You explore ways to make yourself feel more secure about your safety and to protect those whom your care about. In short, you learn how to thrive in the city by knowing how to embrace the energy, the excitement, and the chaos of urban living, but also how to withdraw, retreat and recharge yourself, and, at times, escape.

Staying Safe

While statistics tell us that our cities are becoming safer places to live in, dangers still exist. Becoming crime-smart and street-savvy is largely a matter of knowing what to look out for and then knowing how to avoid it.

Absolutely the best way to avoid trouble in a city is to see it coming before it happens. In order to be able to do this, you need to develop urban radar—you need to be alert at all times. Never become so engrossed in an activity in a public place that you are oblivious to what is going on around you. If you see people just hanging around or acting suspiciously, take note. Be on guard for anything that looks out of the ordinary.

Trust your instincts. Sometimes you've just got to go with your gut feelings. We can often pick things up subconsciously without being fully aware of just what it is we are thinking. Trusting your instincts becomes especially important when you find yourself in poorly-lit areas, deserted streets, or dangerous neighborhoods. If something doesn't feel right, there is a good chance it isn't right. Never go against your intuition in the city—it's your instinct for self-preservation telling you to watch out.

Once you suspect trouble, even a hint of trouble, be evasive —get away from there. Cross to the other side of the street. Walk

TEACH YOUR CHILD THE SAFETY BASICS

Children not only share many of our own anxieties about city life, they also have their own age-related fears. Fortunately, they can be taught much of what adults have sometimes taken time to learn. Probably the best way to prepare them for most eventualities (and without traumatizing them), is through role-playing and acting out some of the situations listed below. Choose only those situations that are suitable for the age of your child/children.

- *Where to go and/or who to contact if they need emergency help.*
- *How to tell someone in an emergency their name(s), who their parents are, and where they live.*
- *How to avoid the hazards of cars and traffic.*
- *How to avoid accidents on their bikes, boards, and skates.*
- *How not to get bitten by people's dogs.*
- *What to do and what not to do when they are home by themselves.*
- *What to do if there is a fire at home.*
- *What streets and areas of the city to avoid.*
- *How to deal with a bully.*
- *How to deal with strangers.*
- *How to deal with a mugger.*
- *How to deal with a flasher.*
- *How to prevent being kidnapped.*
- *How to recognize and deal with a pedophile.*

in the opposite direction. There may be nothing nasty afoot, but it's always better to err on the side of caution. If you find yourself in a part of the city that is eerily deserted, or that makes you feel unsafe, stay on the main roads—don't take short cuts down alleyways however much quicker you might think they will be. Always walk purposefully—you appear less vulnerable if you look as though you know where you are going. Carrying an umbrella also can be a deterrent to potential muggers. Be sure to keep your eyes peeled. And, in the unlikely event that you think you are being followed, hail a cab or go into a store or a restaurant.

Bear in mind that street crime, while it does indeed happen, is not nearly as prevalent as certain media coverage might lead you to believe. However, there is no harm in thinking about what you might do if you found yourself in the unfortunate situation of being threatened. There are no hard-and-fast rules on what to do. Obviously, every situation is different—there are times when you can scream for help, or run, or physically resist. The best advice is: Be very cautious. When threatened with force, most always give the person what he or she wants. No watch or wallet is worth your life. Only resist if you feel that if you do not do so, you will be in greater physical danger.

Crimes are not usually committed randomly. For example, a thief will look for the right opportunity before making his or her move, so don't make yourself an easy target for them. Leave your good jewelry at home, or at least make sure that you keep it hidden when you are in crowded public places. For example, if you are wearing a flashy ring, turn it around on your finger so that the gemstone faces inward; or if you have an expensive camera, keep it in its case, and if possible, disguised within a bag.

If you are in the habit of carrying around a purse, always make sure that you keep it closed—the kind with a zipper is best for this purpose. Be especially careful in restaurants and in other public places, such as theaters and movie theaters. Throwing your purse over your seat can make it easily accessible. If you are sitting at a bar, hold your purse on your lap, and don't leave it on the floor where it can be stolen easily.

Protect your car. Get a car alarm, lock the steering wheel, get an ignition cut-off switch, and if you can't afford parking in a lot, park on a busy, well-lit block. And if you keep things of value in your car, keep them out of sight. Nothing is more attractive to a thief than a laptop or camera lying on the seat. Lock all doors before you leave. Better still, take valuable items with you.

Getting Close to Nature

One of the advantages of living in the countryside, or even in the suburbs, is the ease with which you have access to nature. Non-urbanites are able to laze in their yards, fuss with a petunia, or journey only a few minutes to find themselves surrounded by rural life. Alas, if you live in the city, grass, trees, and wildlife are harder to come by. Yet being in touch with nature is an essential part of finding peace in the city. It can make an incredible difference to the way in which you experience your life there.

City parks have become important features of our urban environment. Hopefully, you live close to a park and hopefully you make use of it. Your local park needn't be anything exotic—just an expanse of grass and trees with a relatively uncluttered vista, offering some respite from the noise of traffic and the hustle and bustle all around you. But even if there is nothing close by, make an effort to get to know the parks in your city.

Most major cities have wonderful parks in the central area—places where you can stroll aimlessly taking in the activity around, or becoming lost in your own thoughts. Many offer great facilities where children can run, play ball, and use the play-grounds, and everyone can walk, sit, picnic, cycle, roller-blade, bump into people they know, or just hang out. And if you are

TUNE IN TO THE NATURAL WORLD

We city-dwellers have become estranged from nature—we are shielded from night by artificial light and insulated from seasonal changes through air-conditioning and central heating. These facilities, while undoubtedly making our lives more convenient and comfortable, also distance us from the Earth's natural rhythms. This exercise helps you to reconnect with nature.

1. Go for a walk in your local park. As you stroll, notice the weather. Is it warm? Is it cold? Is there a gentle breeze or a strong wind? Try to identify any scents, such as freshly-mowed grass, that are carried in the air.

2. Next, take a look around you at the trees, shrubs, and flowers. What stages of growth are they at? Are they in bud or in full leaf/bloom, or just bare? Feast your eyes on the different colors and shades.

3. Now, listen for the sounds of nature. Can you hear birds singing, leaves rustling, or water flowing nearby? Close your eyes briefly and try to recognize as many natural sounds around you as you can.

4. Gently touch some of the flowers, shrubs, and trees. Notice the huge range of textures you find in nature, from the velvety softness of a petal, to the glossy smoothness of a green leaf, to the roughness of a tree trunk.

5. Reflect on the wonder and the beauty of everything around you. Consider your own place in the natural order. Pick up some fallen leaves or petals, and take these home with you to press and keep as a reminder of your connection with nature.

really lucky you'll have access to a park that borders a river or has a lake, where you can watch the sailboats go nowhere in particular, or you can hire a rowboat for an hour or two. Surprisingly, in the city's larger parks you can often find yourself quite alone—one of the few places where there is no one else around. In such surroundings the commotion and stresses of the city can be forgotten—at least for a short while.

If you prefer your contact with nature to be closer to home, you don't need a vast space in order to create your own little urban oasis (see exercise, p.127). If you have even a small yard you could install a little birdhouse to attract wild birds. Look out for wild animals, such as raccoons and foxes, which are flourishing more and more in cities. And don't forget the zoos and aquariums mentioned earlier (see p.128)—they offer an interesting insight into the natural world, and are relaxing places to visit.

If you really like animals, why not get a pet? Conventional wisdom suggests that pets and cities don't really mix; a goldfish or a chinchilla might work, but anything larger is a big mistake. Forget conventional wisdom. If you would like to have a pet, and are willing to devote the necessary time and effort to looking after it properly, get one. This is especially true if you live on your own.

Many city-dwellers say that the best thing that they ever did was get a dog or a cat. Dogs need to go for walks, so they also provide you with instant exercise. And they are great company. Cats, on the other hand, while often affectionate, are more self-contained. They just need access to the outside and they do their own thing. Our family has two cats and I would say that they are quite happy living in the city.

If you join the many urban pet-owners, you will find that your animal is a marvelous antidote to the strains of living in the city. There is now abundant evidence that pets can reduce our stress levels and serve as important sources of comfort. The mere presence of a pet in a room can put us at ease, evoke feelings of caring and tenderness, as well as offer us companionship.

Research shows that stroking a pet regularly can improve our health. Pets can lower our blood pressure and distract us from our own worries and concerns. They can relax us by making us laugh at their antics. Try to play for a few minutes every day with your cat or dog (or ferret, or budgerigar, or whatever creature(s) you share your home with). Even just watching your goldfish can reduce your stress levels and allow you time to regain your equilibrium and restore calm.

Rediscovering Your City

Whenever relatives or friends come to visit us I am reminded of just how wonderful living in a city can be. When they visit it becomes our job to show them around and make sure they have a good time. We take them to see things and do things that we normally never would. And not surprisingly, we begin to get excited about the city again too. Everyone, especially us, has a great time. We always vow to do it again, soon, and without the guests. But alas, we rarely do.

So get out there and rediscover your city! Become a tourist in your own town—even if you have lived there for the last fifty years. See what other people see when they come to your city. Visit all the places that make your city interesting and exciting. No matter how clichéd the attraction, go take a look. (There probably was a very good reason why the attraction became a cliché in the first place.)

Start by buying or borrowing a good map to help you get around. Even before you leave your living room, a map can give you a sense of familiarity and access to your city. Then, start exploring. If you take the car, make sure you park up and do some walking. While cruising around can give you a good overview of which neighborhoods are located where, nothing gets you closer to life in a city than walking around in it. The best way to get to know a neighborhood, new or old, is to stroll along its streets. Walking allows you to control the speed and rhythm of your journey. You are able to luxuriate in all the glorious details, be it the façade of a building, a shop window, or simply the interesting face of a passer-by.

If you would like to do some background reading about your city, try going to your favorite bookstore and heading for the travel section. Most of the moderate to larger city bookstores carry a good selection of books about their own city. Guidebooks these days are far more inviting and fun to read than the dull, dry, versions of yesteryear.

One great way of discovering the interest and excitement that your city offers is to take a mini-vacation right in the center. In most cities hotels offer special weekend deals at prices far lower than the usual rate. Check your newspaper or on the internet as to where the bargains are, choose an appealing hotel, and check in. Get all that tourist information hotels have lying around and ask all those questions tourists are supposed to ask. Then start exploring, doing all the things you normally never would. Discover the city as only someone who lives in that city can.

Then, when you get back home, continue to explore your city by going beyond the usual guidebook and tourist stand-bys. Get to know it on a deeper level. Do some research, ask around, and check out any recommended places of interest. Or choose a specific neighborhood and spend a day exploring just that area. That way, you'll get to find out where those marvelous, off-the-beaten-track restaurants are located, and which of the smaller galleries, museums, clubs, and shops are worth repeated visits.

Usually, the more you know about something, the more you like it. Local libraries are often a great source of information and may have a section on local history. When you know something about the history of a place, a building, a neighborhood, it becomes more meaningful to you and you become more connected to it. The history need not be of the "high-school" variety. It could be a literary history, describing which notable writers and authors lived when and where. Or a social history showing you which performers, artists, movers, and shakers, lived in the city at various times. Your neighborhood feels somehow different knowing that a favorite writer or celeb grew up only a few blocks away. You may never look at those streets and buildings in quite the same way again.

GET OFF THE COUCH

The less you make use of the city, the less pleasure and satisfaction you'll derive from it. You might think that you do make full use of its amenities, but you could be missing out. To find out, take a minute to complete this exercise. Simply check off when was the last time you did each of the activities described below.

The activity	*The last time I did this*
• Went out for dinner	_____
• Had lunch out with friends	_____
• Went out to a movie	_____
• Went dancing or to a night-club	_____
• Saw a play or a dance performance	_____
• Heard a concert	_____
• Went to a sports event	_____
• Visited a museum or an art gallery	_____
• People-watched	_____
• Strolled in the park	_____
• Went shopping just for fun	_____
• Explored a new neighborhood	_____

Your score

If you came up short, and find that you haven't done much to enjoy your city recently, resolve to change this. Pick several of the activities on the list and commit to giving them a try. Schedule them into your calendar over the next few weeks and invite some friends to join you. I guarantee that you won't be sorry.

Savoring the Smaller Pleasures

When we think of the things that bring us the most pleasure in life, we usually come up with the big stuff, such as getting married, having a child, getting a job promotion, or taking a once-in-a-lifetime vacation. While these are wonderfully satisfying and worthwhile events, they happen too infrequently to sustain us on a day-to-day basis. We need something to look forward to or to get excited about more often.

Unfortunately, we tend to take for granted the smaller satisfactions and enjoyments that regularly punctuate our lives. Yet, much of our happiness actually comes from these small morsels of pleasure. They are the individually not-so-terribly-significant involvements and activities that can insulate you and protect you from the bigger stresses of city life. Mine would include having my first cup of coffee in the morning, reading the newspaper, or walking by the park on my way to the subway. I call these small, simple pleasures my "hassle insulators." What are yours? Take a pen and a sheet of paper and make a list of your own. Then, try to think up additional ones that can add to the quality of your life. In case you are having trouble thinking up things you can do to add interest and satisfaction to your life in the city, to follow are some suggestions.

- Find a sidewalk café in your neighborhood and dawdle there.
- Have a meal at an outdoor restaurant.
- Banter with a store clerk, if only for a few brief moments.
- Spend a couple of hours in the public library.
- Sit on a park bench and watch the people go by.
- Cover up and go for a walk in the rain.
- Buy yourself some flowers.
- Buy an ice cream or a frozen yogurt on the street.
- Buy a hot dog from a local street vendor.
- Have a cup of coffee in a coffee bar and read a newspaper.
- Strike up a conversation with a stranger.
- Listen to a street musician (and give him/her a small reward).
- Go walking or jogging in the park.
- Go for a swim in your local pool.
- Browse in a flea market.
- Go to a street fair.

The possibilities are limited only by your imagination. Each can bring a spoonful of joy and happiness to your life. And, when you put them together, such simple pleasures go a long way toward making you feel good about yourself and how you live in the city. Sometimes that can make all the difference.

Discovering Urban Getaways

There are times when the city can overwhelm even the most dedicated urbanite. While we may relish the stimulation, the excitement, and the intensity of city life, occasionally we would relish a break from it. You could compare it to eating too much rich food—from time to time even the most sophisticated of palates craves something bland. So sometimes we need to escape from the city, so that we can continue to appreciate living there. Getting away once in a while provides balance and contrast. It gives you time out to put your city life in perspective.

While there is nothing wrong with an annual vacation—perhaps to a beach in the Bahamas, or skiing in the mountains, or to Disneyland—it's not enough. A better idea is to take more frequent, shorter trips and mini-vacations. Think of time away as your safety-valve that needs to be opened from time to time.

Start by assuming that there is no perfect time for you to get away. You just have to schedule some time off in your calendar, so block out several smaller time-periods when you plan to be away. Do this as far in advance as possible, to insure that you will actually get way. Now you don't have to find the time, it's built-in.

There are short getaways and longer getaways. In order for an escape to be short, you have to be able to arrive at your destination in two hours or less. The plan is to get out of the city for a few hours or a full day and return that same day. Every city offers day excursions via public transport to places and sites just outside its margins. You would be amazed at how much there is to see and do—and is do-able in a day or less.

One of my family's favorite short trips out of the city is to visit a state park and forest about an hour away. In the middle of the park is a lake where you can rent canoes and small sail boats by the hour. We usually bring a picnic and barbecue something or other. It's a wonderful day away.

If you like to get away under your own steam, you might consider cycling. While many people habitually cycle in the city, others are wary of doing so because of all the traffic and the pollution from exhaust fumes, but taking to the open roads might hold greater appeal. Once you get past the city margins, stick to minor roads and before you know it you will find yourself amid great scenery and little traffic. If escaping by pedal-power is not for you, why not strap your bikes onto a car-rack and head out to a national park where you can follow special trails?

Another good short trip you can make is a visit to a farm in the countryside, where you can buy, and even pick, your own fresh produce. As well as milk, eggs, and vegetables, you can often pick apples, blueberries, strawberries, and raspberries at different times of the year. Many farms also offer activities, such as horseback-riding and cider-tasting. If farms are not for you, you might prefer one of the many small country inns or rustic restaurants where you can feast on home-cooked specialties. Meandering through country roads and byways you can sometimes stumble across unique hideaways and remote bed-and-breakfast accommodation that provide the ideal contrast to the size and busyness of the city.

If you live within a couple of hours' reach of the ocean, a day at the shore can be a wonderful escape from the city. Even if the water is too cold for swimming, strolling along the beach or a promenade near the water can be marvelously relaxing.

There are times when you may need to get away for a few days. These mini-vacations can be as simple or as ambitious as you like—a long week-end trip to another country, a few days at a spa or a resort nearer to home. With a little effort you can find inexpensive rates, particularly if you go during an off-peak period.

Wherever you go, have fun, relax and enjoy yourself. But be sure to come back. Your city needs you!

BUILD A GETAWAY FILE

If you are going to escape from the city, you need to know where to escape to. It's amazing how little we know about great destinations that are just an hour or two away from our city. This exercise will show you how to build a getaway file so that you can get the most out of your breaks. You will need a pen, some paper, a file, and a divider, so that you can have two categories: one for trips of one or two days' duration, and a second for longer trips.

1. Start in the travel sections of your local bookstore and library. There are guidebooks describing all manner of trips, places to stay and things to do and see. The kinds of places you might wish to keep information on could include: farms; country inns; bed-and-breakfast accommodation; restaurants; county fairs; mansions and estates that are open to the public; vineyards; botanical gardens; public gardens; nature conservancies; national parks; ski resorts; beach resorts; health spas, and so on. Make notes on the places that catch your attention.

2. Scan newspapers and magazines for suitable articles and visit your local travel agent to collect some brochures. You can peruse these at your leisure, and cut out anything of particular interest to your file.

3. Ask friends, family, and colleagues for recommendations about where to go and what to do. And look on the internet for new ideas. Research about one place might lead to discoveries about others. Before long you will have a comprehensive guide to your own ideal getaways, and you will never be at a loss for somewhere to go to.

Further Reading

800 Ways to Find Peace in a Busy Day, Duncan Baird (London), 1999

Benson, Herbert *The Relaxation Response*, Random House (New York), 1992 and Random House (London), 2000

Brewer, Sarah *Simply Relax*, Ulysses Press (Berkeley, California), and Duncan Baird (London), 2000

Burns, David *Feeling Good*, Avon (New York), 1999

Davis, Martha *The Relaxation and Stress Reduction Workbook*, New Harbinger Press (Oakland, California), 1997

Elkin, Allen *Stress Management for Dummies*, John Wiley & Sons (New York), 1999

Elkin, Allen *Urban Ease*, Plume (New York), 1999

George, Mike *Learn to Relax*, Chronicle Books (San Francisco), and Duncan Baird (London), 1997

George, Mike *Discover Inner Peace*, Chronicle Books (San Francisco), and Duncan Baird (London), 1999

Kabat-Zin, Jon *Wherever You Go There You Are*, Hyperion (New York), 1994

Wilson, Paul *Instant Calm*, Plume, (New York), 1999

Index

Contact the Author

If you would like to contact Dr. Elkin, he can be reached at:

The Stress Management & Counseling Center,

110 East 36th St., Suite 1–C,

New York,

NY 10016

USA